GÖNGU-HROLF

TRANSLATED BY
HERMANN PÁLSSON AND PAUL

Canongate

EDINBURGH

1980

First published in the United Kingdom by
CANONGATE PUBLISHING LTD,
17 Jeffrey Street,
Edinburgh EH1 1DR,
Scotland

ISBN 0 903937 95 6 cased
ISBN 0 903937 96 4 paperback

First published in Canada and the United States by
University of Toronto Press,
Toronto and Buffalo

ISBN 0-8020-2392-4

The publishers acknowledge the financial
assistance of the Scottish Arts Council
in the publication of this volume

UNESCO
COLLECTION OF REPRESENTATIVE WORKS
ICELANDIC SERIES
This work has been accepted in the Icelandic Translations
series of the United Nations Educational, Scientific, and
Cultural Organisation (UNESCO).

Set in Linoterm 10 over 13 Bembo by
Hewer Text Composition Services and printed
by Lowe & Brydone Printers Ltd, Thetford, Norfolk, England.

Contents

Introduction

GÖNGU-HROLFS SAGA is the work of a 14th century author whose name is no longer known. Like so many other story-writers in medieval Iceland, where people were always more interested in the tale than in the teller, he was awarded with the ultimate accolade his grateful readers could bestow: total anonymity. Indeed any work of art, whether verbal or visual, was generally regarded with greater respect than the mind and hand which created it; minor considerations, such as an author's identity, were not allowed to interfere with the sheer pleasure of a well-told tale. The continuous popularity of *Göngu-Hrolfs Saga* since medieval times is easily explained: it is essentially a romance of adventure, an unashamedly escapist kind of literature; its obvious qualities include a well-constructed plot, an interesting cast of heroes and heroines, villains and scoundrels, and a series of exciting events, some of them shrouded in mystery, which generate a sense of suspense throughout the narrative. As soon as the reader finds himself plunged into the hypothetical situation in legendary Russia in the opening chapters he is caught by a powerful current and swept along an intriguing course until every obstacle and hazard lie safely behind and the hero has reached the calm waters of a happy and satisfactory ending.

There is no need to make the point that the Icelanders did not invent this literary genre; rather we are dealing with one of the most enduring forms of narrative art. Like other romances, *Göngu-Hrolfs Saga* follows a basic conventional pattern, and in order to grasp its features it will be useful to consider the genre in broader terms. One of the world's leading authorities on literary theory, the Canadian critic Northrop

Frye, has argued that 'as soon as romance achieves a literary form, it tends to limit itself to a sequence of minor adventures leading up to a major climacteric adventure, usually announced from the beginning, the completion of which rounds off the story'. This major adventure he calls "the quest", and then he continues with his definition: 'The complete form of romance is clearly the successful quest, and such a completed form has three main stages: the stage of the perilous journey and the preliminary minor adventures; the crucial struggle, usually some kind of battle in which either the hero or the villain or both, must die; and the exaltation of the hero. . . . The enemy may be an ordinary human being, but the nearer the romance is to myth, the more attributes of divinity will cling to the hero and the more the enemy will take on demonic mythical qualities. The central form of romance is dialectical: everything is focussed on a conflict between the hero and his enemy, and all the reader's values are bound up with the hero.'[1]

What we propose to do first is to examine the structure of *Göngu-Hrolfs Saga* in the light of these observations of Northrop Frye, and see how far the narrative pattern conforms to the scheme he claims to be characteristic. We can divide the story into five sections, the first of which establishes the potential quest-situation before the introduction of the hero:

I. *The maiden-in-distress* (chapters 1–3). The scene is set in Russia where King Hreggvid of Novgorod fights heroically but unsuccessfully against the overwhelming forces of King Eirik, a sinister viking leader aided by berserks and sorcerers. Inevitably Hreggvid is killed (though his ghost still has a role to play) and the focus shifts to his daughter, Princess Ingigerd. In her distress she temporarily brings out Eirik's better nature. He falls in love with her and makes a vow (the first of many vows and promises that are crucial to the narrative structure) that he will grant her any request she may wish to make. She asks for three years to find a man to fight Eirik's champion, Sorkvir, and promises to become

---

1. Northrop Frye, *Anatomy of Criticism*, New York 1967 (first published in 1957) pp. 186–7.

Eirik's wife if she fails. To this Eirik agrees, though he soon reveals his true nature by resorting to trickery, on the advice of his principal counsellor, a sorcerer and demon called Grim Aegir, in order to prevent anyone getting the dead Hreggvid's armour, without which Sorkvir cannot be defeated. This section prepares the way for the quest which the hero, Hrolf the Tramper, is soon to undertake: the rescue of Ingigerd and the destruction of King Eirik and Grim Aegir.

II. *The minor adventures of the hero* (chapters 4–11). The scene shifts from Russia to Norway and Hrolf is introduced. He is hardly a promising figure at first, the conventional layabout son who has far to go to attain true heroic stature. He leaves home under a cloud, and after disposing of a number of vikings and other villains he reaches the court of Earl Thorgny of Jutland, one of the focal places of the narrative. He becomes a close friend of Thorgny's son, Stefnir, and helps defeat a viking raider from Scotland called Tryggvi, who escapes but is later to reappear. Two strangers, Hrafn and Krak, are introduced next, and are made to look foolish by Hrolf and Stefnir at a ball game, as a result of which they become very surly. But Hrolf acts with courtesy towards them, and they are reconciled with a gift of fine clothing, after which the strangers vanish from Jutland, though like Tryggvi they have a further role in the tale. Now the serious business of the quest begins. Earl Thorgny learns about Princess Ingigerd and makes a solemn vow to aid and win her, but it is actually Hrolf who undertakes the mission and sets out for Russia.

III. *The perilous journey* (chapters 12–27). Up to this point the hero has always been victorious, no matter what the odds against him, but now he is faced with more formidable obstacles, involving threats more complex and sinister than mere physical violence. At a supernatural level, he is exposed to destructive demonic powers, and at a human level to lies, cunning, and unscrupulousness. Before long he comes face to face with the latter, for on his way he meets a man called William who is to plague him throughout much of his quest. William pleads to enter Hrolf's service, but he is a thoroughly unprincipled trickster and traps Hrolf into a vow reversing their roles: William becomes the master and Hrolf his servant. In Russia, the pair of them help Eirik fight off an invasion by Menelaus, King of Tartary, Hrolf doing the fighting and William the talking. Hrolf performs three formidable tasks for which William takes the credit: the capture of a wonderful stag, the entry into Hreggvid's supposedly impregnable burial mound, and the defeat of Menelaus' champion, Soti. For his 'exploits' William wins Gyda, King Eirik's sister, as his wife. Hrolf is now free from his obligations to William; he proceeds to defeat Sorkvir, and then goes off secretly with the Princess. Realising William's deceit, Eirik threatens him, and William makes a vow to kill Hrolf and bring back Ingigerd. He follows them and when he catches up he insinuates himself back

9

into his old job as a servant. As might be expected, he betrays Hrolf again at the first opportunity and leaves him to die, having cut off both his legs, while he himself takes Ingigerd to Jutland. He has extracted a vow from her that, in return for her life, she will say nothing about what he has done to Hrolf. It is growing clear by now that she is in love with Hrolf, but he remains as stolidly unamorous as he has been naive over the unscrupulous William. A further complication enters the narrative at this point. A malicious dwarf, Mondul, tricks Earl Thorgny into believing that his chief adviser, Bjorn, is a traitor, Mondul takes over Bjorn's wife and property and keeps Bjorn a prisoner in his own house. William arrives and recounts his great exploits to an admiring court and a silent and suffering Ingigerd. Meanwhile Hrolf, aided by his faithful horse Dulcifal, makes his way without legs to Bjorn's house. There he overhears what has happened to Bjorn, captures Mondul and forces him not only to restore Bjorn's wife and possessions, but also to graft his severed legs back on. He then goes to Thorgny's court, denounces William and the section ends with William forced at last to tell the truth – he turns out to be a goatherd who has murdered his whole family – and suffer execution.

IV. *The death struggle* (chapters 28–33). Ingigerd delays her marriage to Earl Thorgny by reminding him that her father King Hreggvid has yet to be avenged, and so once more Hrolf volunteers and sets out for Russia, this time aided by Mondul, who has sworn to be loyal to him. After they have left Jutland, the Scottish viking Tryggvi turns up once more and kills Earl Thorgny; Bjorn retreats to the stronghold at Aarhus and two mysterious strangers help the army defeat Tryggvi. Now the story returns to Russia where, in a ferocious and in some respects absurd three-day battle, Hrolf confirms his heroic stature and the usurper King Eirik is killed along with his demonic retinue, with the aid of Mondul's witchcraft and the strong arms of two mysterious strangers, who characteristically turn up exactly when needed.

V. *The exaltation of the hero* (chapters 34–8). Only one stranger survives the battle and he now reveals himself as Hrafn, one of the two brothers treated with courtesy by Hrolf earlier in the story. But there is a further revelation to come: it turns out that his real name is Harald, son of King Edgar of England whose throne has been seized by a usurper. All these revelations are made at a feast celebrating the funeral of Earl Thorgny. Hrolf, now the proven hero, agrees to help Harald, so they set off for England where they defeat the usurper, after which they return to Denmark and a triple wedding feast is held, described in lavish and enthusiastic detail. In due course Hrolf goes back with Ingigerd to rule over the whole of Russia. *Hrolf the Tramper* ends with geographical information about England and Denmark, a brief account of the sons of Hrolf and Ingigerd, and an epilogue on the nature of the story and of storytelling, which will be considered below.

10

It should be clear from this summary that the narrative conforms in essentials to Frye's pattern for romance fiction. Later we shall try to go beyond this formal aspect and look at some of the details that give the story its own particular life. The overall structure is not the only conventional feature of the story; it contains a number of other elements which recur frequently in hero legend and romance, such as the sword of chastity, the helpful horse, the magical protective garment and the sleep-thorn. The stag hunt in chapter 13 characteristically leads the hero through a wood and into a clearing where he comes face to face with an elfwoman living in a mound – for similar episodes, see *Gautrek's Saga*[1] (ch. 1), *Egil and Asmund* (ch. 11), *Thorstein Mansion-Might* (chs.3 and 4). A helpful character with supernatural powers will heal an amputated limb as Mondul does in ch. 25 and Eagle-Beak in *Egil and Asmund* (ch. 14). Like the hero of *Arrow-Odd*, who has to deal in battle after battle with Ogmund Eythjof's Killer, Hrolf has an elusive enemy, Grim Aegir, who can dive into the earth as easily as into water. The dead Hreggvid continues to lead his weird existence in the grave mound, as do Aran in *Egil and Asmund* (ch. 7) and Gunnar in *Njal's Saga* (ch. 78). Hrolf and his blood-brother compete against surly opponents in a ball game, which has a striking analogue in *Bosi and Herraud* (ch. 3). Earl Thorgny's habit of mourning his wife by sitting on her grave mound is paralleled in *Gautrek's Saga* (ch. 9) and *Hrolf Gautreksson* (ch. 1). Typical actions, such as battles, tournaments, single combats, and banquets, are described in essentially the same terms as elsewhere in the literature, as indeed are individual characteristics. 'Good-looking and intelligent daughters' keep turning up as 'the best match in Scandinavia'; and berserks typically 'look more like trolls than human beings', and are endowed with a skin that 'no sword will bite', unless the sword happens to be enchanted and to belong to the villain himself. The maiden-in-

---

1. For translations of literary texts referred to in the Introduction and in footnotes to the story, see *Bibliography*, pp. 127–8. below.

11

distress held captive by a malevolent ruler is common enough in romance, and it is interesting to note here that Ingigerd's own sufferings are reflected on a smaller scale by those of Thora, daughter of Earl Thorgny. The three usurped thrones – those of Hreggvid, Thorgny, and Edgar – comes as no surprise either, and the recurrence of the number three serves to strengthen our confidence in the author as a writer of romance: there are three tasks to be performed by the hero at King Eirik's court, three days of crucial battle against Eirik and Grim Aegir, three visits of the hero to Russia, as untested youth, as questing warrior, and as triumphant king; Hreggvid emerges three times from his grave mound, Ingigerd has three years to find her champion; and there are various other instances of the structural significance of the number three. Yet another device of the narrative pattern is the recurrent use of spells, vows, choices, and prophetic warnings, the stuff of which the formal aspect of romance constituted.

As we have attempted to indicate, *Göngu-Hrolfs Saga* is by no means an artless and loosely-constructed work. The author is always conscious of his noble role as a storyteller and fully aware of the narrative discipline he so cheerfully accepts; indeed he has the grace to remind us of it from time to time, as for example when he comes up against the vexed problem of keeping several narrative strands under control:

> Now the story returns to the point where we left it, for it's not possible to tell two stories at the same time, even though that may have been the way they happened. (78)

So at times he will introduce figures who may seem scarcely relevant to the main plot, then banish them from it in a deceptively offhanded way, only to reintroduce them later; he is invariably master of his puppet characters, and the reader is not let into the secret of the show until every string has served its purpose. Thus we read about the two young men at the court of Thorgny, Hrafn and Krak, who seem at first no more than casual visitors to the tale, introduced only to reveal the

12

superior skill and courtesy of the unlikely hero. They accept his gifts of clothing very grudgingly and appear then to have served their function; but they re-emerge later, at first unidentified, as the mysterious strangers who aid Thorgny's men against the viking Tryggvi, and then Hrolf in his crucial battle with Eirik. The revelation of their identities as 'Hrafn' and 'Krak' creates a link with the earlier part of the tale, but the surviving brother's further revelation of 'Hrafn' as merely a cover for his true identity, Harald son of King Edgar of England, is the means by which the author is able to send Hrolf off on his last adventure as fully accredited hero, before he actually becomes ruler. The reappearance of the sinister Tryggvi of Buchan in Scotland not only allows the author to reintroduce the mysterious strangers, but also enables him to get rid of Thorgny and so open up the way for Hrolf's marriage to Ingigerd.

The vow, or oath, is yet another structural device to give the story its ultimate form, serving a thematic function: the keeping of oaths is associated with the preservation of the social order, while their violation leads to social and moral disintegration. Eirik, in love with Ingigerd, swears an oath allowing her to stipulate whatever she wants; she makes the formalised choice – three years of waiting and the ritual of challenge – and Eirik at once reveals his fundamental dishonesty by resorting to the trickery and magic proposed by Grim Aegir in an effort to render Ingigerd's choice virtually ineffective. Hrolf and Ingigerd, on the other hand, observe their own vows to the letter when these are given to William, even though they know William can be trusted only to break his vows and promises. In the black-and-white moral world of the tale, Hrolf and Ingigerd have to win against the heavy odds of sorcery and treachery used against them by Eirik and William, the unholy alliance of treachery and power, doomed to failure because, for all their difference in rank, they share the worst of all vices: bad faith. On the other hand, an apparently evil figure, Mondul the dwarf, shows himself a man of his word when he swears to help Hrolf and does so. Consequently the author lets off this potentially evil character lightly compared with his treatment of William. There is something tongue-in-cheek about the author's comment on Mondul as he leaves the stage for the last time. Having helped Hrolf to victory against Eirik, the lechery of his earlier villainies is presented in a less sinister light:

> King Eirik's sister Gyda vanished from Russia, and some people have guessed that it must have been Mondul who carried her off. (114)

Gyda, it will be remembered, had been married to William as a reward for his great 'exploits' in Russia.

As must have become apparent, the storyteller himself is an important 'character' in the story and, as we shall argue below, some assessments of this and similar narratives have been inadequate because they have failed to take this sufficiently into account. Much of the virtue of the story lies in the skill with which the narrator blends the unlike (and often unlikely) material he draws upon, and it must be emphasised that his aim was radically different from the kind of 'realism' we find in the more famous sagas on native Icelandic themes, such as *Njal's Saga*, as indeed the author himself indicates in his pseudo-scholarly remarks on some of the more outlandish events. For example, when the dwarf Mondul Pattason grafts Hrolf's legs back on several weeks after they have been cut off, the authorial comment runs:

> Now even if people think such a thing incredible, it's still everyone's responsibility to say whatever he's seen or heard. And it isn't easy to contradict what has been said in the past by men of learning. Had they wished, they could surely have told a very different tale if it had happened any other way. Then there are wise men who have written figuratively – men such as Master Gualterus in *Alexander's Saga* and the poet Homer in *Trójumanna Saga*. Masters who have come after these have vouched for the truth of what was written, and not denied that things might have happened that way. No one however need take it as literal truth when he can just listen to the story and enjoy himself. (84–5)

This adaptation of the mask of naïveté in a confrontation with learning can be recognised again during one of the set-piece battles:

14

Sturlaug saw the great damage Thord was doing him, what with his men nearly routed and a number of them dead. He sought out Thord, who turned to meet him, and a long bitter combat followed between them before Sturlaug could land a blow. It caught Thord on the pate and the sword proved as good as ever, for it split his head wide open and went straight through the trunk so that he fell to the ground in two halves. But Sturlaug had gone too far this time, for his short-sword shot down deep into the earth and was never seen again. As to these events, books don't agree at all. According to *Sturlaug's Saga* and other tales as well, Sturlaug died in his bed at home in Ringerike and was buried there in a mound, but here it's stated that after Thord's death Grim Aegir came up out of the ground behind Sturlaug and sliced him through with a sword. We can't say which comes nearer the truth. (101–2)

In fact the narrator begins and ends with a lively personal commentary on the business of storytelling and pleasing audiences, and his characteristic tone is brought out in his final paragraph:

So here we must end this tale of Hrolf Sturlaugsson and his great exploits. I'd like to thank those who've listened and enjoyed the story, and since those who don't like it won't ever be satisfied, let them enjoy their own misery. AMEN. (125)

To its teller the story is unashamedly and entertainment, though with a few winks at the great tradition it looks towards its own serious moral ends:

Since neither this tale nor anything else can be made to please everyone, nobody need believe any more of it than he wants to believe. All the same the best and most profitable thing is to listen while a story is being told, to enjoy it and not be gloomy: for the fact is that as long as people are enjoying the entertainment they won't be thinking any evil thoughts. Nor is it a good thing when listeners find fault with a story just because it happens to be uninformative or clumsily told. Nothing so unimportant is ever done perfectly. (2)

These amiable disclaimers provide us with both a frame to and an internal commentary on the content of the tale, and it would be a heavy-handed critic who would insist on any strict comparison with

Njal's Saga or *Eyrbyggja Saga*. As we have seen, the narrative structure is deliberately, emphatically conventional, the content fantastic, often absurd, and the author knows it to be.

Elements of the absurd are present in the tale by the author's own choice as well as by the convention of romance. Even the hero is not exempt. Hrolf is seen by his father as better fitted for the quiet life than for heroic enterprise and there remains a trace of the bumpkin about him despite all his feats of arms. There is something grotesque about his great size; we are told that he was so heavy 'there wasn't a horse could carry him all day, which is why he always travelled on foot'. Even when we learn that he liked 'to practice at the butts and joust on horseback' there's the qualifier that 'he was so heavy and so powerful that no one could budge him from the saddle but he was clumsy with weapons and never carried them. Most people found him harmless and inept'. Much of this is there, of course, to be disproved by his future actions, but it has a grain of truth in it. 'Look around for a wife and settle down on a farm', advises his father. 'Get yourself a croft in some out-of-the-way valley . . . and live out your life as best you can'.

> 'I've no mind to become a farmer' said Hrolf, 'and I don't mean to marry. I've no use for women.' (37)

When Hrolf's father offers him ships and men,

> 'I can't be bothered to haul people along behind me', said Hrolf. 'They might start missing my brothers' company. And don't talk to me about fighting. I can't stand the sight of blood. And I don't like the idea of cramming myself into any of those little overloaded boats either – they might sink and drown the lot of us.' (37)

Of course, at this point Hrolf is deliberately playing the clown, but though the course of the story reveals his courage and skill, something of the stubbornness and stupidity his father accuses him of remains a part of his nature, particularly in his persistent failure to see through the absurdly transparent William, and in his inability to recognise how

16

Ingigerd feels about him. The trouble seems to go beyond the sleep-thorn when, lying beside Ingigerd, the sword of chastity between, he can't be woken:

> Ingigerd got up and tried hard to rouse Hrolf but couldn't wake him, no matter how much she tried. She left the shelter and burst into tears. When William saw this, he asked didn't she enjoy sleeping with Hrolf?
> 'I like everything about him,' she said, 'but he's sleeping so fast that I can't wake him up.'
> 'I'll wake him,' said William.
> Going up to the shelter, he tore it apart and cut off both of Hrolf's feet, then hid them under his coat. Hrolf slept on undisturbed. (80)

Of course, Hrolf is the honest and good-natured man deceived by the vicious William, and a virtuous man too, bringing home the distressed maiden to his lord, Earl Thorgny, even though she prefers Hrolf, but there is at the same time a touch of absurdity about the proceedings recognised by the author as an aspect even of the most virtuous conduct.

In William, on the other hand, we might discover affinities to Falstaff. He is so gross and palpable in his sycophancy and unscrupulousness that he takes on comic proportions. Figures of this kind are likely to be acceptable only if presented as absurd and once they are recognised as constituting a serious threat they are characteristically, like Falstaff, rejected or destroyed. So in the early stages of the story William has something of the appeal of a Falstaff on, or immediately after Gadshill, alternating between grotesque self-inflation and fawning obsequiousness. Here he is at the court of King Eirik:

> This was at the time of day when the king was at table. They greeted him, and he gave them a friendly reply, asking them who they were.
> 'I'm called William and this fellow with me is my servant Hrolf,' said William.
> 'I'm an earl's son from Friesland but I had to make a quick getaway after my own people had tricked me out of my inheritance. I've come here because I've heard all about your splendour and magnanimity and I'd be glad of your hospitality over the winter.'

'I won't begrudge you your food', said the King. 'I take it you're a great sportsman?'

'I'm master of a good many skills', said William. 'For one thing, I'm so tough, my strength is inexhaustible. I can outrun any animal, quadrupeds and all.'

'A useful talent for thieves,' said the King, 'but one that often comes in handy.'

'I'm not short of talent when it comes to shooting or handling weapons either,' William continued, 'or swimming, or chess, or jousting, or learning and eloquence. If there's anything that lends grace to a man, I've got it.'

'I can see you're not exactly backward in coming forward either,' said the King. (55–6)

At this level, William is a lively comic creation on the author's part, as he is too in his other 'character', fawning upon the upright and over-trusting Hrolf whose horse Dulcifal,[1] as it happens, understands William better than he does since William 'could never come anywhere near Dulcifal, for the horse would bite and kick him whenever it got the chance.'

'I've suffered terribly since we parted,' said William. 'The King had me thrown into a dungeon and even wanted me killed; but starving and frozen stiff as I was, my cunning saw me through. Now I'm at your mercy, dear Hrolf, you can do just what you like with me but I promise never to do anything to upset you again, and I'll be loyal and faithful to you for ever, as long as you spare my life and let me go back to Denmark with you.' (79)

Within a page, William has cut off the sleeping Hrolf's legs and is on top of the world again, and it is at this point that he is no longer quite so funny. Even when Hrolf was performing William's tasks for him at the court of King Eirik, at least William compensated somewhat for his public boasting with his private praise of the hero, and functioned more as clown than villain since it was clear where the heroic talents really

---

1. The name of this horse derives ultimately from that of Alexander the Great's famous steed Bucephalus which in early Balkan versions of the legendary history of Alexander has the form 'Douchipal'. See F. P. Magoun, Jr., "Whence Dulcifal in Göngu-Hrolfs saga?" in *Studia germanica tillagnade E.A. Kock* (1934), pp. 176–91.

lay. The parallel with Falstaff is relevant at this point. In *Henry IV i*. Falstaff functions very much as court-jester and as an ironic foil to the larger-than-life heroics of Hotspur. But in *Henry IV ii*. his conduct grows increasingly callous as he shows indifference to other men's suffering and death and is concerned with little but his own immediate advantage. The cutting off of Hrolf's legs has something of the same brutality about it, and prepares the ground, in so far as the narrative is morality, for the downfall and summary execution of William, who was, we learn, the murderer even of his own family:

> That, in so many words, was the death of William, and it was no more than was to be expected that such a vile man should come to such a vile end, traitor and murderer that he was (88)

The events of the story at a literal level, are of course often crudely bloodthirsty and this is a feature that some readers have found little to their taste. The problem however might be seen to lie in an over-literal reading of the tale, against which the author's explicit warning has already been quoted. Fundamentally, the tale is not intended as a reflection of ordinary life, but sets up tensions between a conventional and moralistic plot on one hand, and an extravagant or comic-grotesque manner of presentation on the other. Many times, and quite emphatically in his Prologue and Epilogue, the author makes the reader aware of the tongue-in-cheek manipulation of the narrative, and the events have more in common with mock-epic, Antigonus pursued by a bear, or even a Tom and Jerry cartoon, than with the imitation of life found in realistic narrative art. The massive carnage of battle, for instance, simply cannot be taken seriously nor does it appear to be so intended, for the number and manner of the deaths are inflated to such grotesque proportions that the stark heroisms of the great 'realistic' saga tradition are seen to have undergone a crazy transformation. The characters are unmistakeably typical – Hrolf the clean-cut, clean-living country boy; Grim Aegir the eminently hissable demon king; William an ultimately sinister *miles gloriosus* whose life in the tale arises not from realism but from comic exaggeration; Ingigerd the helpless maiden and Eirik the villainous king with the maiden in his power – we have seen them all before. But in the end we must come back, not to the bare materials of the author but to the way in which he manipulates them. This is a subject we shall revert to in our closing paragraphs, but at this point we wish to stress once more how little the author draws upon a known, common life or the history of his own and earlier ages.

We have remarked before that the tale is seen by its author as essentially an entertainment, one might almost say escapist fiction, though there is rather more to it than such an expression might imply. The world of magic was alive in folklore, but had roots in a mythic past. So the principal demon, Grim Aegir, has as the second element of his name that of the old sea god, meaning 'ocean'. Similarly, the horse Dulcifal shares something with Sigurd's Grani, and helpful creatures like him occur elsewhere in romance narrative. The sword of chastity is another common enough element, playing a vital role in *Volsunga Saga*, and in the heroic poetry of Scandinavia. And though the viking element blended with the mythic has some historical basis the age of vikings had ended over three hundred years before the story was written, and as we have said its presentation in this genre is deliberately stereotyped. Closer to contemporary experience would be the element of courtesy and courtly elegance drawn from the southern literary tradition. Nevertheless, while the description of the great wedding feast is a far cry from the magical monstrosities and bloodthirsty events found elsewhere in the tale, it is still done in terms of wonder and spectacular extravagance:

> They spared nothing on halls and furnishings or anything that was to be found in Scandinavia. To this banquet they invited burghers and courtiers, counts and earls, dukes and kings and everyone of any standing. Most of the nobility in Denmark were there, and when all of them had arrived and been shown to their seats, there were courteous young squires and the finest gentlemen to attend on

them. All kinds of dishes were served there, spiced with the most precious herbs, and every sort of game and wild fowl, venison from deer and reindeer, pork from the best wild boars, geese, ptarmigans, and peppered peacocks. There was no shortage of glorious drinks, ale and English mead, and the best of wines, both spiced and claret. And once the wedding and the banquet had begun, all kinds of stringed instruments, harps and fiddles, pipes and psaltery, were to be heard. There was a beating of drums and a blowing of horns, with every variety of pleasant play to cheer the body of man. After that the two young ladies were escorted into the hall with a colourful train and cluster of splendid women. Two noblemen led by the hand each of the two ladies who were to marry the bridegrooms. Above them, supported on painted poles, was a canopy to conceal their resplendant clothing and elegance until they were seated. When the canopy was taken away, no colour, it seemed, could outshine their complexions, their skin, their gleaming hair and all the glowing gold and jewels that they wore. Yet when they saw Ingigerd, everyone thought Alfhild and Thora pale by comparison. The banquet was held in all splendour, and during the feast Hrolf married Ingigerd, Stefnir Alfhild, and Harald Thora. The feast lasted seven days without a break, everything being arranged as we've just described; and it ended in honour and magnificence. (121–22)

It might be said that this tale, like many romances, has two distinct trends. One of these reveals a world of desire or wishfulfilment, such as in the description of the banquet, or the dreamlike invulnerability of the hero. The other element, derived from folklore and myth, is that of magic and reveals a world of mystery or fear, or of supernatural wonder, dealing as it does with the unkown. As with most romance tales, once the hero travels beyond the elegant walls of the court, the stylized and spectacular, but still credible life of ladies and knights gives way to situations in which nothing is certain, men can suddenly turn into monsters, and the hero gropes his way through woods and along paths that appear to be not of this world. The history and geography of romance fiction is characteristically blurred and the authors of this fiction are fascinated by faraway places with strange-sounding names, though in fact the author of this particular tale uses a geography more limited than many of the genre. *Arrow-Odd* for example ranges between

'Slabland Waste' (Labrador), 'Giantland', a mythical country in the north, and south as far as the Mediterranean. The heroes of *Egil and Asmund* are aided by a Queen Eagle-Beak who has been to visit King Snow in the underworld, against a gang of giants from Jotunheim. *Bosi and Herraud* takes the heroes to Glasir Plains, the home of the ambiguous king and demi-god, Godmund. The author of Göngu-Hrolf however shows a rather more precise sense of geography and even some scraps of historical knowledge too, though nothing very exact. His information is sometimes weirdly exotic, as in his observation that the horse Dulcifal evolved from the dromedary, and he will sometimes introduce a piece of information into the middle of one of his character's speeches, as when Hrafn offers us this snippet on Scotland:

> Henry had a lot of support from Scotland, being married to the daughter of Earl Melans of Moray, a close friend of Duncan, High King of Scotland, who founded Duncansby, and gave it his name. (115)

The author's reference to the River Dvina in Russia shows a similar desire for precision as he halts his narrative briefly to inform us that it is 'the third or fourth biggest in the world, and it was to find its source that Yngvar the Far-Travelled set out, as told in his saga.' He can use pseudo-history for comic effect, as in his speculations on the death of Sturlaug quoted above, but his account of England reads like a brief encyclopedia entry and seems to come straight out of a geography lesson:

> England is the most productive country in Western Europe, because all sorts of metals are worked there, and vines and wheat grow, and a number of different cereals besides. More varieties of cloth and textiles are woven there than in other lands. London is the principal town, and then Canterbury. Besides these there are Scarborough, Hastings, Winchester, and many towns and cities not mentioned here. (122)

Immediately after this comes another geographical 'entry', this time on Denmark and again a neat and accurate summary:

Denmark is a very disjointed country. Jutland, the largest part, lies southwards bordering on the sea. Jutland Side is the name of that part lying on the west coast from Skagen south to Ribe. There are several important towns in Jutland, Hedeby being the most southerly; another is Ribe, a third Aarhus, and Viborg a fourth, where the Danes choose their kings. Limafjord lies in Jutland stretching north to south, with Harald's Isthmus separating the head of the Fjord from the sea to the west. That's where King Harald Sigurdarson had his ships hauled across when he was fleeing from the attacks of King Svein. West of Limafjord lies Skagen curving northwards, its main town being Jellinge. Between Jutland and Fyn stretches the Little Belt; the capital of Fyn is Odense. Between Fyn and Zealand is the Great Belt. Roskilde is the main town on Zealand. North of Zealand lies the Sound, and to the north of that, Skaane, with its main town of Lund. Between Jutland and Skaane are several large islands, Samso, Anholt, Laaland and Langaland. The isle of Bornholm lies east in the Baltic. At that time the Skjoldungs ruled over this kingdom, and even though other kings and earls had realms just as large as theirs in Denmark, the Skjoldungs were held in greater respect because of their title and family.[1] (122–23)

As for history, a number of names in the saga appear to come from historical sources, though they have little to do with their originals. The name of the hero is also that of the Scandinavian leader, son of Rognvald Earl of More, and ancestor of William the Conqueror:

> Earl Rognvald's second son was Ganger-Hrolf, who conquered Normandy: the earls of Rouen and kings of England are descended from him. (*The Book of Settlements* ch. 309; see also *Orkneyinga Saga* ch.4, 'Ganger-Hrolf. . . . was so big that no horse could carry him. . .')

The names Duncan and William also echo English, Scottish, and Norman history and the Battle of Ashington (ch.36) dimly recalls the actual battle which took place in 1016. Allusions to English history are borrowed from *Knytlinga Saga* or *History of the Kings of Denmark* which mentions not only Ashington, but also Brentford and Winchester, where King Knut (Canute the Great) and his son Harald were buried.

---

1. The geographical information here derives from *Knytlinga Saga*, a 13th century history of the Kings of Denmark from c.950–1140.

The most interesting parallel with history occurs in the account of the invasion of Russia by King Menelaus of Tartary (chs. 17–18). This echoes chapter 238 of *King Hakon's Saga* (in *Flateyarbok*) which describes how King Alexander of Novgorod sent messengers about the middle of the 13th century, as he was interested in Hakon's daughter as a possible wife for his son. Hakon sent his own messengers and reached Novgorod just as the Tartars were attacking Alexander, as a result of which the marriage proposals fell through.

But it is clear that the historical elements of the story are fragmentary and rarely exact; and where the geography is accurate it only plays a minor and occasional part in the narrative. Like other romance fiction, *Göngu-Hrolf's Saga* is in this respect very different from the fact-based (though by no means strictly historical) sagas on Icelandic themes. For this reason romance fiction has often been downgraded on the grounds that, comparatively speaking, it lacks the sophisticated sense of character and motive or the social realism of the more famous saga tradition. Significantly, the great sagas rose in popularity in the 19th century, in which the novel became the major European art form in literature. We have tried in our introduction to present a case for viewing and evaluating romance fiction in its own terms and not simply as the degenerate offspring of *Grettir's Saga* or *Eyrbyggja Saga*. The problem is in some respects not unlike that facing the student who comes to Shakespeare's late plays after immersion in the great tragedies. Commentators on Shakespeare have often had difficulty with, for example, *The Winter's Tale*. Pope thought so little of it that he was reluctant to admit Shakespeare's hand except for a few passages, and for Lytton Strachey it showed Shakespeare to be 'bored with people, bored with real life, bored with drama'. Phrases such as 'afterthoughts to the tragedies' or 'that absurd pot-boiler' are not uncommon[1], and unsympathetic critics can point to the apparent absence of the psychological realism commonly

---

1. See J. H. P. Pafford (ed.) *The Winter's Tale* (1966) pp.xxxvii–xliv.

claimed for the great tragedies, the arbitrariness with which Mamillius and Antigonus are disposed of and Autolycus is introduced, the crazy shifts of time and place, the whimsical geography that gives Bohemia a sea coast, the mingling of tragical, comical and pastoral materials, the absurdity of Hermione's twenty-year vigil, the incredibility of her statuesque reappearance and her reconciliation with Leontes. And yet to say this would be to ignore the play's own particular form and purpose, to see it not as a play but as a 19th-century novel, or as a Jacobean tragedy not a romance. The tendency has been for critics of Shakespeare to move firmly towards a more sympathetic view of the late plays whenever these have come under attack and to point, as Pafford's edition does, to the 'mistaken standards of consistency or taste' of those who dislike them. Without wishing to claim for Icelandic romance fiction the same status as late Shakespearian romances, we still wish to point to a similar need, to examine the romances not in the light of other Icelandic narrative forms, but in terms of their own imagined worlds.

ACKNOWLEDGEMENTS

The text used in this translation is from Guoni Jónsson's *Fornaldarsögur Norourlanda*, Reykjavik 1959, which is based on a 15th century vellum MS; a critical edition of all extant MSS is yet to be attempted. We should like to thank Professors Robert Kellogg and Paul Schach for their help and encouragement, and Mr Robin Lorimer for his careful editing of the volume as a whole.

Edinburgh, July 1978

Hermann Pálsson   Paul Edwards

Key Characters

Hreggvid, King of Russia
Ingigerd, his daughter
Eirik, a sea king, usurper of the throne of Russia
Gyda, his sister
Sorkvir, Brynjolf,
Thord, Grim Aegir } King Eirik's berserks and champions
Sturlaug, ruler of Ringerlike in Norway
Hrolf (the Tramper), his son
Thorgny, Earl of Jutland
Stefnir, his son
Thora, daughter of Earl Thorgny
Bjorn, Earl Thorgny's counsellor
Ingibjorg, wife of Bjorn
William, a farmer's son in Denmark
Menelaus, King of Tartary
Soti, his leading champion
Mondul Pattason, a dwarf and sorcerer
Tryggvi, a berserk from Buchan in Scotland
Vazi, his blood-brother
Melans, Earl of Moray
Duncan, High King of Scotland
Harald, son of King Edgar of Winchester
Sigurd, brother of Harald
Alfhild, their sister
Henry, a kinsman of Edgar and usurper of his throne. (son-in-law of
    Earl Melans).

26

GÖNGU-HROLFS SAGA

Prologue

O F THE MANY stories written for people's entertainment, a number come down to us from ancient manuscripts or from learned men. Some of these tales from old books must have been set down very briefly at first, and expanded afterwards, since most of what they contain took place later than is told. Now not everyone shares the same knowledge, and even when two men happen to be present at the same event, one of them will often hear or see something which the other doesn't. Moreover there are plenty of people so foolish that they believe nothing but what they have seen with their own eyes or heard with their own ears – never anything unfamiliar to them, such as the counsels of the wise, or the strength and amazing skills of the great heroes, or the way in which powerful magic, sorcery and witchcraft may bring death or a lifetime of misery to some, yet bestow wordly honours and riches and high rank on others. At times, these sorcerers would stir up the elements, then calm them down again, just like Odin and all those who learnt magic and medicine from him.[1] There are actual cases of dead bodies moving about under the control of an unclean spirit, for instance Eyvind Split-Cheek in *Olaf Tryggvason's Saga*, Einar Cormorant, and Frey who was killed in Sweden by Gunnar Half.[2]

---

1. In *Ynglinga Saga* and elsewhere Odin is described as a master-sorcerer who taught his art to others and could even control the elements.
2. Eyvind Split-Cheek was one of the principal adversaries of King Olaf Tryggvason who during his five year reign (995–1000) waged a ruthless war on paganism and paved the way for Christianity in Norway. Einar Cormorant figures in *Heimskringla*. There is an amusing story about Gunnar Half telling how he destroyed an image of the god Frey and then impersonated him during a fertility rite, fathering a child on the priestess in attendance.

Since neither this tale nor anything else can be made to please everyone, nobody need believe any more of it than he wants to believe. All the same the best and most profitable thing is to listen while a story is being told, to enjoy it and not be gloomy: for the fact is that as long as people are enjoying the entertainment they won't be thinking any evil thoughts. Nor is it a good thing when listeners find fault with a story just because it happens to be uninformative or clumsily told. Nothing so unimportant is ever done perfectly.

CHAPTER 1

King Hreggvid

THERE WAS ONCE a king called Hreggvid, who ruled over the state of Novgorod, which some people call Russia. He was big, strong, and very handsome, brave and skilful in battle, wise in his counsel and generous to his friends, but harsh and ruthless when it came to his enemies, in every way a man of outstanding gifts. His Queen came from a very noble family, but her name isn't given and she doesn't enter our story.

King Hreggvid and his Queen had an only daughter called Ingigerd. She was the loveliest and most courteous woman in Russia and even beyond, and wiser and more eloquent than anyone else in the land. She had mastered all the feminine arts that were practised far and near at that time by nobly-born women. Her hair was as fair as gold or cornstalks, and long enough to veil her whole body. The King was very fond of his daughter. She had her own house in the town, well situated, solidly built, and elegantly ornamented with gold and precious stones, where she would spend the day in the company of her women.

King Hreggvid was then getting on in years, but the story tells how in his younger days he used to spend much of his time fighting. He'd won territory beyond the River Dvina that flows through Russia; from there he'd raided various nations to the east and taken from them many a rare treasure. This river is the third or fourth biggest in the world and it was to find its source that Yngvar the Far-Travelled set out, as told in his saga.[1]

King Hreggvid spent seven long years on this expedition, but when people thought he must be dead, he came back to Russia and settled down. He'd got himself a stallion called Dulcifal which understood human speech. In size and strength, Dulcifal wasn't to be compared with any other horse, for he was as swift as a bird, as nimble as a lion and as strong as a wolf. If defeat lay ahead for the one who was to ride him, no one could ever get hold of Dulcifal, but if there was victory to come he would go straight to his master.

King Hreggvid's armour was the only set of its kind. The helmet was covered with precious stones, and so strong that it was impossible to destroy. His mailcoat was of the hardest steel, treble-plated, and it shone like silver. The shield was far too broad and thick for any iron to bite and the lance which went with it was hard and tough, and would ring out like a bell when struck against the shield. If it didn't ring out, defeat was sure to follow. His sword never faltered in a stroke, and a charm had been laid on it so that it would bite steel and stones as easily as if they were soft flesh. It was made of grey iron[2] (from a fjord called Ger), which will neither crack nor rust. Dulcifal was of a special breed of horse related to the dromedary. Since King Hreggvid had got this

---

1. *Yngvar's Saga* is attributed to the monk Odd Snorrason (late 12th cent.) but was probably written much later. It is still extant. This Yngvar was an historical figure and belonged to the first half of the 11th cent. According to the Icelandic Annals he died in 1041. He is said to have worked as a missionary in Russia and about 30 runic stones in Sweden commemorate the names of people who accompanied him to the east. *Yngvar's Saga*, however, is largely legendary and of slight historical value.

2. *grey iron* (gerjarn); the translation is doubtful, as is the identification of the fjord *Ger* with which this word is associated.

horse and armour, he'd never suffered a defeat. There was plenty of fighting going on in the kingdom, for he and his men were always engaged in great battles.

The King had a number of counsellors and other eminent men about him. One of them was called Sigurd, nicknamed Wool-String, the grandson of Halfdan Red-Cloak, son of Kari the Singed. Sigurd was a man of great courage and liked by everyone, but he was growing old. He'd seen long service with the King and had helped him loyally in all kinds of danger.

CHAPTER 2

The sea king and his berserks

THERE WAS A king called Eirik, a sea king. His family belonged to Gestrekaland, which is ruled by the King of Sweden. People there are strong and troll-like, hard, ugly men to deal with, and full of witchcraft. King Eirik was a big, powerful man, with swarthy big-boned features. He used to lie at sea summer and winter alike with a large fleet, plundering in many a country. He was a great fighting man and utterly ruthless. Much of the time he had his good-looking sister called Gyda staying with him.

In his army Eirik had a large number of beserks and champions, four of them mentioned by name. Two were brothers, one called Sorkvir and the other Brynjolf. They were big and strong and ugly to deal with, sorcerers so brimfull of witchcraft that they could blunt weapons in battle. Sorkvir was the stronger of the two, and a great man at jousting.

The third berserk was a kinsman of Eirik, a big strong man called Thord and nicknamed Laeso-Pate. His family belonged to Laeso Island in Denmark, where he'd grown up. He had a blood-brother called

Grim Aegir, a powerful and thoroughly evil man. No one knew Grim's background or his family, for he'd been found on the beach at Laeso Island by the sorceress Groa. She was Thord's mother, and reared Grim as her foster-son. She taught him so much about witchcraft that no one in Scandinavia could rival him, and his nature was utterly different from any other man's. Some people think that Grim's mother must have been a sea ogress, for he could travel at will in both sea and fresh water; that's why he was called Grim Aegir.[1] He used to eat raw meat and drink the blood of men and beasts. He would often change himself into the forms of various creatures and could do it so quickly that the eye hardly saw it. His breath was so hot that even men in armour could feel it burning them. He could spew venom and fire at people, killing both them and their horses, and they were helpless against him. King Eirik put great trust in Grim and all his other men; and so, unsparingly, they worked away at their evil business.

CHAPTER 3

Hreggvid's death

SO KING EIRIK came to Hreggvid's Kingdom with his army, killing, looting, and burning down settlements. As soon as folk realised they were under attack they went to see King Hreggvid and told him what had happened. He wasted no time, but had the war-arrow[2] sent out, ordering every able-bodied man to join him. But he could gather only a small force, for the enemy had struck so suddenly, and most people had grave doubts about the outcome.

---

1. Aegir means 'Ocean' and was also the name of the sea god in Scandinavian mythology. Stories about the god Aegir are to be found in Snorri Sturluson's *Edda*.
2. *herör*; a token to summon men to war.

In the morning, just before the battle, King Hreggvid put on all his armour; he fastened a precious gold necklace about his throat, and hung his fine sword at his waist. He took the lance and struck it against the shield, but it made no sound, and Dulcifal couldn't be caught. A large number of men chased the horse and eventually managed to pen him inside a deep gulley. The King came up and tried to catch him, but when he saw the King, Dulcifal leapt over the barrier and out into the wood. Everyone thought this very ominous and knew that it meant certain defeat, so they made no effort to go after the horse. King Hreggvid had another brought to him, along with a shield and a lance, and he gave his best shield and lance to his daughter for safekeeping. After that he and his troops prepared for battle.

King Eirik called his army together urging every brave man to do all that he was able, and not to spare his efforts.

"It's no more than our duty, sir, for each to do all he can," said Grim Aegir. "If we defeat King Hreggvid, we want to settle down here. I want the title of Earl and some land to be put in my charge. Your kinsman Thord's to come with me, and we'll share whatever fate decides for us; but Sorkvir and Brynjolf shall go with you and defend your Kingdom."

The King agreed to all that Grim had said, and declared that this was how everything must be. Then both sides formed up, and the two armies began to close on each another, King Eirik leading one flank of his army, and Grim Aegir the other. The odds were so far from equal that there were four of the enemy to every one man in the home army. King Hreggvid advanced against King Eirik, Sigurd Wool-String against Grim Aegir, and the fiercest of battles began, with hewing and slashing, shot and stone. Each army marched up to the enemy ranks shouting and urging their companions forward. Bodies fell tumbling one on top of the other as King Eirik's berserks strode ahead, chopping up King Hreggvid's troops as if they were firewood. Seeing this, Sigurd Wool-String hacked a way right and left through to Thord

Laeso-Pate and swung at him, but Thord put his pate in the way of the stroke, and the sword made not the least impression. Then Thord gave Sigurd his deathblow, and he fell like a true hero.

King Hreggvid saw all this and took the death of Sigurd badly. He spurred his horse forward hard, hacking and hewing to right and left at men and horses, clearing a path through them all. The sword bit everything as if it were slicing through water. Around the hilt it was superbly ornamented in gold, and hidden in the pommel were healing stones which took all pain and poison from wounds rubbed with them. Sometimes cutting down two or three men at a single stroke, both arms drenched with blood to the very shoulders, King Hreggvid rode forward in fury right up to King Eirik's banner. Grim Aegir and Thord struck at him together as he came up to them, but so bravely did the King defend himself that he suffered not the slightest wound. Then Grim began to belch out such a quantity of witchcraft that the King's horse faltered and almost fell. King Hreggvid jumped from its back and hacked away on either hand. He piled the corpses of his victims so high around him that the carnage reached up to his waist. Then with both hands he struck at Grim Aegir, who warded off the stroke with his breath, blowing the sword from Hreggvid's grip. The King grabbed an axe and striking at Thord's pate with the back of it, knocked him out for some time. With a running jump he leapt over the pile of dead. King Eirik came hewing with his sword at King Hreggvid, but it broke at the hilt and didn't bite into the armour. Then Grim Aegir lunged with his sword up under the corselet and right through him. The King fell, bravely with honour; there's hardly a man in Russia more glorious than King Hreggvid.

Most of his army had fallen and all the survivors fled, but a great number of King Eirik's troops had been killed too. Then the flag of peace was hoisted, and those who asked for and were granted their lives came to terms, but those who wouldn't serve King Eirik were put to death; and that's how the battle ended.

Afterwards all the dead were stripped, and King Eirik marched into the town with all his followers, bringing drink and music and every sort of pleasure. So the night went by. In the morning the King summoned Grim and his companions, saying that it was time to call on the Princess, and that's what they did.

The Princess gave greetings to King Eirik when they came to her chamber, though she'd been weeping bitterly and was very distressed. King Eirik tried to comfort her and said he would give her compensation for the losses she'd suffered, in both life and property. 'Any proper request you'd care to make, we'll grant,' he said, 'as long as you'll be reconciled with us and do what we tell you.'

'No one has the right to call himself king if he can't keep his promises to a young lady,' said the Princess. 'I'll agree to do as you say on one condition, that you honour your promise and grant me my request. But I'd rather take my own life than go with any man against my will, and then nobody would enjoy me.'

The King fell deeply in love with her. 'If any man breaks his promise to you,' he said, 'I'll blackguard his name. So make your request, and I'll grant it.'

'This is my first request,' said the Princess: 'a burial mound to be built for my father, spacious and well-appointed inside and surrounded by a high stockade. It's to stand far off in the wilderness, and gold and valuables are to be put in the mound with him. He's to wear his full armour and his sword, and to be seated on a chair with his dead companions on either side of him. None of you is ever to touch his horse – Dulcifal must be left to run free. Then I want to rule over a quarter of the Kingdom for three years, and the men I appoint to govern with me and all those who serve me must be left in peace. Each year I'll try to get someone to joust against you or your champion Sorkvir, and if none of my subjects is skilful enough to knock Sorkvir from the saddle during these three years, you can have me and the entire Kingdom. But if Sorkvir's defeated, you're to leave Russia with all your troops and never come back, and I'll take charge of my father's lands and Kingdom, according to my rights.'

'You ought not to grant her this request,' said Grim Aegir, 'it's been carefully and deliberately considered. I don't think it's right for you, sir, to pay suit for so long to her or any woman. Still, you can rely on Sorkvir, and on my wisdom and advice too, so nothing will go wrong.'

'Princess,' said the King, 'I had no idea you'd make a request like that. But I'll keep my word to you, for I put my trust in Sorkvir. You'll never find a better man than him.'

They sealed their agreement with binding oaths, and with that their talk came to an end.

'I've an idea that's sure to work for us,' said Grim Aegir. 'We must cast a spell, and by sorcery we'll make certain no one can beat Sorkvir, either at jousting or in single combat, without wearing King Hreggvid's full armour. We'll have the mound built so strongly with bricks and tiles that no human being could break into it. You'll want to keep all your promises to the princess, so send men for the armour, and offer your sister Gyda to anyone who gets it. Then they'll either be killed on the quest, or else the armour will be in your hands.'

The King and all his followers thought this an excellent idea, so a mound was raised and King Hreggvid placed inside. Ingigerd was the last to leave the mound. She had secretly brought two sets of armour and laid them on her father's knee. Then the mound was covered up, and all the arrangements were made as Grim Aegir had proposed. After that the Kingdom was divided up according to the agreement, and everything was done as we have described it. The Princess couldn't find anyone who would risk taking on Sorkvir; and although the King sent a good many men to the mound, none of them ever came back.

Grim Aegir became ruler of Ermland, one of the kingdoms in Russia, and those who had to serve him were far from happy about it. Grim and Thord Laeso-Pate kept waging war on the inhabitants of Giantland north of Alaborg. That would be a story worth telling. They kept fighting great battles against one another using magic and witchcraft, but neither side could get the better of the other, and they both ended up losers.

Sorkvir and Brynjolf spent the summers raiding, and were also in charge of King Eirik's defences. Princess Ingigerd settled down quietly with her best men at one of the castles in her kingdom, but she was very worried about her future.

CHAPTER 4

Hrolf sets out

WHILE ALL THAT we've described was taking place, Sturlaug the Industrious was ruler of Ringerike in Norway. He was married to Asa the Handsome, daughter of Earl Eirik, and they had several promising sons. One was called Rognvald, and the second Fradmar, the third Eirik, and the fourth Hrolf, named after Hrolf Nose, Sturlaug's blood-brother, who died in the temple in Ireland when Sturlaug went there to fetch the auroch's horn.[1]

Hrolf Sturlaugsson was an exceptionally big man, tall and sturdy, and so heavy there wasn't a horse could carry him all day, which is why he always travelled on foot. He was the handsomest of men. He didn't mix very much with ordinary folk, and seldom took part in games or entertainments, though he did like to practise at the butts and joust on horseback. He was so heavy and so powerful that no one could budge him from the saddle but he was clumsy with weapons and never carried them. Most people found him harmless and inept. He wasn't like his brothers, and there was always a coolness between him and them.

---

1. This is an allusion to *Sturlaug's Saga*, one of the legendary sagas.

One day, as often happened, Sturlaug and Hrolf were talking together. 'It seems to me you'll never amount to much," said Sturlaug; 'you act more like a woman than a grown man. The best advice I can give you is to look around for a wife and settle down on a farm. Get yourself a croft in some out-of-the-way valley where nobody will ever set eyes on you, and live out your life as best you can.'

'I've no mind to become a farmer,' said Hrolf, 'and I don't mean to marry. I've no use for women. But I can see plainly enough why you're turning against me. You begrudge me the very food I eat. So I'll clear out of here, and I won't come back until my lands are no less than yours: if not, I'll die in the attempt. It strikes me that this place of yours is no better than a croft itself, and far too small to be divided between us brothers. Well, none of you need ever look to me again for help.'

'If you mean to set your mind on something which might earn you fame and respect, I can give you ships and good seamen,' said Sturlaug.

'I can't be bothered to haul people along behind me,' said Hrolf. 'They might start missing my brothers' company. And don't talk to me about fighting. I can't stand the sight of blood. And I don't like the idea of cramming myself into any of those little overloaded boats either – they might sink and drown the lot of us.'

'I'm going to help you with nothing,' said Sturlaug. 'I can see you're stupid, and stubborn as well.' And with that they parted, each of them seeing things his own way.

Hrolf went over to his mother Asa, and said, 'I'd like you to show me the cloaks your foster-mother Vefreyja made long ago for my father.' She did as he asked, and opened a large coffer.

'You can see the cloaks here,' she said. 'They've hardly aged at all.'

Hrolf picked up each of the cloaks, and this is how they were made: they were long and wide, with sleeves and a hood, and a mask to cover the face. Iron couldn't bite them nor could venom spoil them. Hrolf took the two largest.

37

'I'm not getting much from my father's house,' he said, 'if all I'm to have are these cloaks.'

'Surely you can't be in that much of a hurry to leave, my son,' said Asa, 'without weapons or companions?'

But Hrolf walked off without a word, and few days later he vanished. No one knew what had become of him. He bade farewell neither to his father nor to his mother, nor to any of his kinsmen. They had no idea what had happened to him, though it isn't said that Sturlaug troubled himself much over his son's disappearance. So now, for a while, Sturlaug lived quietly in his kingdom.

CHAPTER 5

Earl Thorgny

THE STORY TELLS OF a man called Thorgny. He ruled over Jutland in Denmark, where his residence was, but collected tributes from other lands as well. He was a great chieftain, and had with him the very best of followers. He was getting extremely old when the events of this story took place, and his queen was dead, though two of his children still lived, a son called Stefnir and a daughter, Thora. Both were good-looking and very gifted. Stefnir, the Earl's son, was a man of enormous strength and a great sportsman, but always gentle and even-tempered. Thora was an unusually clever needlewoman, and a boudoir was built for her where she used to sit with her women.

There was a man called Bjorn, the Earl's counsellor and very close friend, wise, benevolent, and skilled in the arts of war. His wife Ingibjorg was a courteous, well-bred lady, and Bjorn loved her very much. He had an estate not far from the town, but he spent most of his time with the Earl.

Earl Thorgny had loved his own wife very dearly too. Her grave mound stood near the town, and the Earl would often sit there when the weather was good, either to hold meetings or watch the games played for him. His kingdom was usually very peaceful, and most of his life passed quietly by.

CHAPTER 6

A Swedish outlaw

NOW WE RETURN to Hrolf, who had set out from Ringerike, as we've already said. Weaponless but for a single oak club, he wore one of Vefreyja's cloaks and carried the other. None of the paths was known to him, and he travelled more through mountains and forests than through settlements. He made his way east to Eida Wood as he wanted to go to Sweden, but he didn't keep to any of the paths through the forest, so he kept losing his way and would wander around for days on end.

Late one evening in spring he came upon a strongly-built house in the forest. The door was shut, but he set down his club against the wall outside and walked in. There was one bed, and some seats standing between the bed and the door. He saw some furs there, but little else of value. Hrolf lit the fire.

At sunset a huge man came into the house, wearing a black coat with a brown hood. His face was swarthy, and his eyebrows joined together, and he was heavily bearded. He had a sword at his waist, and carried a spear.

'Who's this thief?' he asked. 'Where have you come from?'

'There's no reason for you to be so ill-mannered,' said Hrolf. 'Still, I won't bother to keep my name from you, I'm called Hrolf, and I've come from Ringerike.'

'Be damned to the lot of you who come from there!' said the man

39

who owned the house. 'Get away from the fire and up onto the bench. You can take your ease there.'

Hrolf did as he was told, and when he was seated the owner of the house said, 'I'll not keep my name from you any longer. I'm called Atli Otryggson, and my family's from Ringerike. I know all about you. You're the son of Sturlaug the Industrious, and now you can pay for the outlawry your father laid on me after I'd killed one of his retainers.'

And grabbing his spear with both hands, he drove it so hard at Hrolf's chest that it doubled him up, but it didn't bite through the cloak. Hrolf wanted to stand up, but couldn't because he was stuck fast to his seat.

Then Atli said, 'Your witchcraft won't help you much longer. I'm going to get your club and beat you to death'.

With that, he ran out of the house. Hrolf felt things were going badly and struggled hard until the board he was sitting on came loose. At that moment Atli came in with the club. Hrolf threw himself at Atli, who dropped the club. The two men grappled and began to wrestle ferociously. Hrolf went for his man so hard that Atli was forced to give ground and in the end fell flat on his back. Hrolf kept up the pressure and squeezed Atli's neck and throat with both hands. Atli couldn't make a sound, and though he gave Hrolf a hard time of it, Hrolf didn't loosen his grip until Atli was dead.

In the house Hrolf found a lot of money and took it all, along with the sword and spear, but left the club behind. He took the coat off Atli because he thought it lighter for walking in than the cloaks, and these he carried. He burnt Atli's body and stayed there overnight. In the morning he went on his way and walked for days through the forest.

One day he came to a clearing and there he saw eleven fully-armed men. One of them was more finely dressed than the others, and it seemed to Hrolf that this man must be their leader.

When they saw Hrolf, the leader said, 'Atli the Evil's here. Up on your feet, all of you, kill him now and pay him back for his looting and killing.'

Hrolf hadn't time to speak up for himself before they'd set on him furiously, hewing and thrusting. Hrolf took a bold stand, striking or lunging with the spear and landing many a heavy blow, for the spear was a fine weapon, though he himself suffered wounds on his hands and feet. They made a long fight of it, but in the end Hrolf killed them all. He was tired out, and had a lot of minor wounds. He dressed them, then discarded the coat, as he didn't want this kind of thing to happen to him again. It seemed to him that these men must have come from Vermaland, either on a hunting trip or else looking for Atli.

Hrolf went on his way, and there's nothing to tell of his journey until he reached Gotaland, at Gota River, where he saw a ship floating close to land. It was a big longship, with the awnings up from stem to stern. There was a gangway ashore, and above it a fire was burning, where people were cooking their meal. Hrolf let the mask fall over his face, then went up to the men by the fire and greeted them. They returned his greeting and asked him his name and where he'd come from. He gave the name Stigandi and said he'd come from Vermaland. Hrolf asked whose ship this was, and who was their master. They said he was called Jolgeir, and belonged originally to Siljansdale in Sweden.

'Someone like that must be a good man to serve,' said Hrolf.

They said that anyone who served Jolgeir would get the worst of the bargain. 'He's a berserk, brimfull of witchcraft, and iron can't bite him. He's a rough man and hard to deal with. There's eighty of us aboard, but we don't serve him by choice. He killed our leader, who owned this ship; and he's forced us to swear loyalty to him, all through trickery and witchcraft. Now he's planning to go plundering in the Baltic.'

Hrolf told them they'd entertained him well, then he went aboard, walked up to Jolgeir and greeted him. Jolgeir was sitting in the poop, and Hrolf thought there was an ugly look about him. Jolgeir returned the greeting, asking his name, and what he wanted.

'I'm called Stigandi,' said Hrolf, 'and what I want is to serve good masters. I'm quite willing to do anything that needs to be done, but I'm no fighting man. I've heard good reports of you, that you're a great chieftain and a generous man with food to anyone who needs it.'

'You've been told the truth about me being free with food,' Jolgeir said, 'but I don't like your looks: you strike me as dangerous. Still, you can join us if you want.' Hrolf thanked him, and their talk came to an end.

That summer they went on a viking expedition. Hrolf kept giving the men silver from Atli's purse, and everyone except Jolgeir came to like him. To him, Hrolf seemed to be no better than a layabout, who slept a lot, did no work aboard, and never risked himself in any fighting or danger. Jolgeir plundered quite ruthlessly, usually robbing farmers and merchants. He plundered mostly in Courland and collected plenty of loot.

On one occasion Jolgeir told Stigandi to keep watch aboard ship. It was lying close in with a gangway ashore. The weather was foul, with rain and a gale blowing. The crew went to sleep, while Hrolf stood watch at the head of the gangway. The night passed, but by morning Hrolf had become drowsy and had wrapped himself up in Vefreyja's cloak. Jolgeir woke up, put on his armour and walked ashore carrying a sword in his hand. He saw where Hrolf was lying fast asleep, snoring by the embers. Jolgeir flew into a rage, raised the sword, and using both hands struck at Hrolf's waist. The stroke would have killed him, had the cloak not protected him. The blow woke Hrolf up and he jumped to his feet, while Jolgeir tried to strike him again, this time on the head. Hrolf went for Jolgeir, who was ready for him, and a fierce fight began between them. Jolgeir kept pressing Hrolf hard, but he retreated, backing towards the sea, until they both plunged down over a cliff and into the water. Each tried to hold the other under, and for long they stayed submerged. Many a time they plunged deep down. Nobody chose to join in the struggle, though everyone favoured Hrolf.

Eventually the two stopped fighting and made their way back to the shore, where Hrolf managed to scramble to his feet. It shelved very steeply to a sheer drop below the waterline. Hrolf stood waist deep, but Jolgeir couldn't touch bottom. Hrolf grabbed him by the shoulders, held him underwater, and kept him there till he drowned.

Then Hrolf went ashore, utterly worn out. Every one of Jolgeir's men thanked him for what he'd done and said what a great man he was to have defeated such a dangerous berserk.

'I suppose you'll want to have me as your leader now instead of Jolgeir?' said Hrolf. 'Well, I'll not treat you any worse than he did. Now I want to tell you honestly who I am: my name's Hrolf, and my father's Sturlaug the Industrious, who rules Ringerike in Norway.'

They all cheered him and said his background was noble enough, so no wonder he was such a great champion. Then they held a meeting at which they decided formally to become Hrolf's men and to accept him as their ship's captain. Hrolf was free with Jolgeir's loot and paid them generously, so it didn't take long for him to become very popular. They fought a good many battles, and Hrolf won them all.

That autumn they sailed back west again, and Hrolf said they should head for Denmark, where they arrived late in the autumn, not far from Earl Thorgny's residence, in Jutland. They sailed into a secret cove, secured their ship, and put the awnings up.

Hrolf told his men to wait for him there till he got back. 'I'm going ashore by myself to see what's happening here,' he said.

CHAPTER 7

Hrolf visits Thorgny

THE STORY GOES that one day when Earl Thorgny was at home in Jutland sitting at the drinking table, the hall door opened, and a stranger walked in, a big, heavily-built man, wearing a long fur cloak, and carrying a spear in his hand. Everybody inside marvelled at his size. He went up to the Earl and gave him a respectful greeting. The Earl returned it and asked who he was.

'I'm called Hrolf, and my father's Sturlaug who rules Ringerike,' he said. 'I've come here to see how you live. They tell me you're a great chieftain.'

'I know all about your family and background,' said the Earl; 'and I'm glad to welcome you to my country. You can have any favours you'd care to ask for, as long as they're fit to be granted. How many men would you like to have in attendance daily?'

'There are eighty men aboard my ship,' said Hrolf; 'and I want them all to accompany me. I've plenty of money to pay our way. I'd like to have a castle not far from you where I can keep my men; and, if you like, I'll willingly defend your country.'

'I'm very glad you've come,' said the Earl. 'You can have anything that you think will add to your reputation.'

Hrolf thanked the Earl for his offer, and went back to his men. The Earl put them in charge of a castle, where Hrolf took up residence, living a quiet life and entertaining his men lavishly. But he also spent a good deal of his time fighting, and defended the Earl's kingdom vigorously. Stefnir and Hrolf became fast friends, and Bjorn the Counsellor was on close terms with Hrolf as well. So time passed, but nothing happened worth mentioning.

CHAPTER 8

Battle with berserks

THERE WAS A man called Tryggvi, Ulfkel's son. His family came from Buchan in Scotland. He was a great warrior and berserk, and used to lie out at sea summer and winter with a large fleet. He had a blood-brother called Vazi, a real troll in both size and strength. Thorgny had killed Tryggvi's father when he was on a viking expedition. By this time Tryggvi had acquired twelve ships, all of them well-manned and well-armed, and with this fleet he sailed to Denmark to take revenge on Earl Thorgny for his father. Vazi and good many other warriors were with him.

As soon as they landed in Earl Thorgny's country, they began to create havoc, plundering the settlements, killing people, and looting everything they could lay their hands on. When the Earl heard about this, he had the war-arrow sent out and mustered his forces, but since he was getting on in years he appointed Hrolf and Stefnir leaders of the army. This was Hrolf's second year in Denmark.

Hrolf and Stefnir set out to meet Tryggvi with ten ships. The encounter took place near some uninhabited island. They didn't waste any time on formalities, and at once the fighting began. Tryggvi and Vazi had a big dragon-headed longship, and were formidable enemies. The dragon ship was hard to attack because of its height, and its crew kept pelting stones down on Hrolf and his men. Many of them were killed and others wounded, so that the battle began to go against them, but Stefnir and Hrolf were wearing Vefreyja's cloaks, and there wasn't a weapon could hurt them. Then they laid their ship alongside the dragon and attacked it fiercely. Hrolf had Atli's spear and carried a massive oak club under his belt. Stefnir carried a good sword, and was the best of warriors.

45

In the thick of battle, Hrolf leapt aboard the forepart of the dragon ship, and went hard at the enemy, thrusting with his spear so fiercely that the men in his way who weren't knocked flat were skewered upon it. Stefnir followed close on his heels striking out to right and left, and before long they'd completely cleared the forepart of the deck. Then they made their way aft, one on each side, with the enemy all backing off towards the mast. By now it was late in the day.

When Tryggvi and Vazi saw how things stood, they went back on the attack, Vazi with a halberd in hand, and Tryggvi an axe. Hrolf took on Vazi, and each made a thrust against the other. The halberd caught Hrolf's shield, splitting it right through, though Hrolf wasn't hurt. Vazi took Hrolf's blow on his shield, but the spear glanced off into his thigh, making a great gash. While Vazi hacked at the spearshaft, Hrolf grabbed the club to defend himself, hitting out at Vazi's shield and smashing it to pieces. So the fight went on, and it was a long time before Hrolf managed to break the shaft off the halberd. Then Vazi threw himself at Hrolf, almost knocking him flat. Hrolf dropped the club and grappled with him so long and hard, it seemed to him that, apart from men in a berserk fit, he'd never wrestled with anyone stronger. In the end however Hrolf managed to inch him over to the gunwale and broke his back on it.

All this time, Stefnir and Tryggvi had been fighting too; with sheer weariness, and with all the blows he had taken, Stefnir was on his last legs, but was still unhurt, whereas Tryggvi was badly wounded. Hrolf hurried over to them, and as soon as Tryggvi saw him, he dived straight overboard without bothering to wait. It was too dark to search for him, and by this time the battle was over. All the survivors were spared, but there were six ships on either side without a man left aboard. They took a great deal of loot there, and then they went home.

The Earl thanked Hrolf handsomely for all the fighting he'd done. For the time being there was no sign of Tryggvi and that was how Hrolf and Tryggvi parted.

CHAPTER 9
Hrafn and Krak

IT HAPPENED ONE day, as indeed it often will, that two strangers came into the hall. They were sturdy and tall, but shabbily dressed and poorly armed. When they went up to the Earl and greeted him, he responded cheerfully and asked them their names.

'We're brothers,' said the taller of the two. 'I'm called Hrafn, and this is Krak. We're Flemish.'

'They must have been short of good names,' said the Earl, 'when they gave those to brave fellows like you.'[1]

'We'd like hospitality over winter,' said Hrafn; 'we've been told you're friendly towards strangers from far away.'

He said they were welcome to stay and told them to take seats down from the foreman on the middle bench. The Earl treated them generously, but they took no part in the fun and games with the others. Ball games were often played there, and people kept urging the brothers to join in. The brothers said time was when they'd played a very hard game. The Earl's men replied that no matter how things went for them, they were quite capable of looking after themselves.

One morning the brothers joined in the game, and had the ball most of the day. They kept pushing the other players around, hitting out at some and knocking them flat. In the evening three had broken arms, and a good many others were bruised and maimed. The Earl's men felt they'd been given a rough time of it. After things had gone on like this for some days, they asked the Earl's son, Stefnir, to join in the game and try to level the score for them.

---

1. *Hrafn* means "raven", and *Krak* (Krákr) "crow" or "rook".

47

Stefnir agreed, and went over next morning to the playing field. When Hrafn saw him, he said. 'Are you really so tough they won't let you play anyone else? Or is it that you think yourself such a big man that no one will dare play against you?'

'I'm not too strong to play nor too arrogant either,' said Stefnir.

'Then I challenge you to a game in three days' time,' said Hrafn. 'You can choose any other man you like to play against me and my brother, if you dare to play at all.'

'You can be sure I'll come and play you,' said Stefnir.

Then he went off, got himself a horse, and rode over to Hrolf's castle. This was during Hrolf's second year in Denmark. When Hrolf heard Stefnir had come he went out to meet him and after he'd given him a warm welcome they sat down to drink.

'I'll tell you why I'm here,' said Stefnir: 'I want you to join me and play my father's winter guests, Hrafn and Krak.'

'I'm told they're strong men,' said Hrolf, 'and that they've maimed several folk, and even killed a few. I know nothing about games, but if it's what you want, I'll go with you.'

After that they went back to town, and the Earl gave Hrolf a friendly welcome. Next day Hrolf and Stefnir went over to the playing field, where the brothers were already waiting. Hrafn picked up the ball, and Krak the bat, and they started playing their usual game. The Earl was sitting on a stool watching. When they'd been playing for a while, Hrolf managed to get the ball, then snatched the bat from Krak and gave it to Stefnir. After that, they carried on playing for quite some time, and the brothers weren't able to get the ball.

It happened that as Hrafn was running after the ball, someone put a foot in the way, tripping him up. This practical joker was a young kinsman of the Earl. Getting to his feet in a rage, Hrafn took hold of the man who'd tripped him, lifted him in the air, and threw him down so hard that his neck broke. The Earl called to his men to take Hrafn and kill him. Hrolf rushed up to Hrafn and grabbed hold of him, while nearby, Krak and Stefnir began grappling with each other too. Hrolf would stand for no interference. They hadn't been wrestling long before Hrolf lifted Hrafn against his chest, then threw him down flat, scraping the skin off his shoulders and knocking him unconscious.

When Hrafn came to, Hrolf went up to him. 'I can see, Hrafn, that you've the look of a nobleman,' he said, then turned to the Earl. 'I implore you, sir,' he said, 'spare the lives of these men, for I know they're well-born.'

Stefnir who had beaten Krak, asked his father to let Hrolf have his way. The Earl's anger was a long time cooling, but he decided to spare the men's lives as Hrolf and Stefnir had pleaded. The brothers walked off very stiffly back to their room without a word and didn't appear at table that evening.

That was the end of the game, and everyone went off to drink. Hrolf spoke to Stefnir. 'Take the finest cloth we have,' he said, 'and give it to your sister Thora, so that she can make clothes for the brothers. She's to have them ready early tomorrow morning.'

So that's what Stefnir did – he went to Thora with the cloth, handed it over, gave her the instructions and left. She set to work at once. Night passed, and early in the morning Thora sent the finished clothes to Hrolf. He took them and went over to the brothers' room, where they were still in bed.

'Why is the raven so late on the wing?' asked Hrolf. 'The eagles and other birds of prey have had all they want but there's still plenty of carrion left.'

'It's hard flying for a wounded bird with broken feathers,' said Hrafn.

Hrolf took the clothes, threw them over to the brothers, and went away. The brothers picked them up, put them on, and went to table. Winter went by. It's not mentioned that Krak and Hrafn even thanked Hrolf for giving them the clothes or for saving their lives, though the brothers were well treated. At the beginning of summer they vanished suddenly, and though no one knew what had become of them, many thought there was something very odd about the way they'd acted.

In the summer Hrolf went on a viking expedition, and Stefnir with him, taking plenty of loot and making quite a name for themselves. They came back home in the autumn safe and sound, but nothing is said of their exploits.

CHAPTER 10
A solemn vow

HROLF SPENT THE summer highly honoured by Earl Thorgny. One day in autumn, as Thorgny was sitting on his Queen's burial mound watching the game that was being played for his entertainment, a swallow came flying above him, dropped a silk scarf onto his knee and then flew off. The Earl picked up the scarf, and when he untied it, there inside was a human hair, the length of a man and the colour of gold. That evening, the Earl went back to the drinking table and showed people the hair the swallow had dropped. Everyone agreed it must be a woman's hair.

'Whichever woman this hair belongs to,' said the Earl, 'I swear a solemn vow to win her or die in the attempt, once I find out the town and country where she lives.' People were impressed by the vow, and exchanged glances with their neighbours.

Some days later the Earl convened a great assembly. He got to his feet and made public his solemn vow, asking if anyone knew anything about this woman, and where she might be found. The hair was handed round, in case someone should be able to identify it.

Bjorn the counsellor spoke: 'I would hope, sir,' he said, 'for my words and deeds to enhance the honour and standing of your Kingdom, not reduce it to shame or suffering. To me, your vow seems a most solemn thing. I don't think you're fated to win this woman, but I can make a sound guess at where she is, though I've never made enquiries about it. A king called Hreggvid used to rule over Russia. He had a daughter called Ingigerd, the loveliest and most gifted woman in every respect. I've been told without a word of a lie that there's not a woman in Northern Europe with greater gifts or with hair more luxuriant and fair, and I believe that no matter how strangely you came by this strand of hair, it must be hers. You must surely have heard that Hreggvid was killed by King Eirik and what happened to the Princess? She has to get a man to joust with the King's champion, Sorkvir, and there's no other way she can save herself, but considering the man they'd be up against, I don't think there'll be many volunteers. Even if someone should manage to knock Sorkvir out of the saddle, in my opinion it won't be easy to get the Princess out of Russia.'

Everyone there agreed that what Bjorn had said was no less than the truth.

CHAPTER 11

A journey promised

EARL THORGNY was silent for a while after Bjorn's speech, and then he spoke.

'Anyone who's willing to go to Russia,' he said, 'joust against Sorkvir and so win this girl on my behalf, to him I promise the hand of my own daughter Thora and a third of my Kingdom as well. I'll be generous with both ships and seamen to any man willing to do this.'

Everyone went very quiet at these words, and no one answered the Earl until Hrolf stood up.

'It's hardly polite,' he said, 'to make no reply to such a leader as we

51

have. I've been staying with you, sir, for some time now, enjoying generous entertainment and many favours, so I'll undertake to go on this mission and try to win you the Princess, or die in the attempt. Should I come back from these travels, you're still free to marry your daughter to anyone you like. She deserves a good husband but, for myself, I've no mind to take a wife.'

The Earl thanked Hrolf handsomely and told him he could have as many men as he wanted, but Hrolf said he didn't want anyone with him. 'A lone traveller creates less suspicion than a great crowd,' he said.

Stefnir offered to go with him, but Hrolf wouldn't hear of it, and so the assembly came to an end. Hrolf went back to his castle, and everyone else to his own home.

CHAPTER 12

William

SHORTLY AFTERWARDS HROLF vanished from the castle, leaving all his men behind, and no one had any news of him. He was wearing Vefreyja's cloaks, with Atli's spear as a stick, and a bow and quiver on his back.

What route Hrolf followed isn't known, but when he was almost out of Denmark he happened one day to see a man coming towards him. The man was tall, armed from head to foot, and carrying a drawn sword in his hand. He came up to Hrolf, who greeted him and asked him his name.

'I'm called William', he said, 'but I won't waste time on my background. You've a choice before you: either tell me who you are, where you're heading, and what's your business, or I'll kill you on the spot and that will be the end of your travels.'

'No need to give me such a hard choice,' said Hrolf. 'However things may go, my prospects are no worse than yours'.

William lunged at him with his sword, but Hrolf warded it off with his spear and wasn't harmed. Then he dropped the spear and set on William, who grappled with him. After some time William went down.

'Now I can do whatever I like with you,' said Hrolf. 'You'd better tell me your mission and where you come from.'

'My family's from Denmark,' said William, 'and I'm a farmer's son. I was planning to go to Russia, break into King Hreggvid's mound, get his armour, and win King Eirik's sister Gyda, but now I'd like to be your servant. I've some good points, I'm a smart fellow and well-spoken. You'd do best to spare me, I'll serve you faithfully and be a great help to you.'

'You're a good-looking fellow,' said Hrolf, 'and I don't want to kill you, as long as you promise to serve me. I don't trust the look in your eyes, though.'

So Hrolf told him to get up, took him into his confidence, and explained the object of his journey. Then they went on their way. William's horse was there close by. William hated having to go on foot loaded with weapons, and his clothes and saddle gear showed how fond he was of finery. So it was William who led the way as they travelled through Denmark.

CHAPTER 13

Treachery

ONE DAY THEY saw a fine impressive farm building.
'We can spend a comfortable night here on this farm,' said William. 'It's owned by a kinsman of mine called Olvir, a good farmer with plenty of servants.'

As they rode up to the great house, the farmer came out to meet them. He welcomed William cheerfully, and Hrolf too, asking who that big fellow could be.

'He's called Hrolf,' said William, 'and he's my master. He's a big strong man, well-born, and a great champion.'

The farmer invited them to have a drink. There were a good many freedmen there, but William wouldn't trust anyone other than himself to serve Hrolf, and all the time kept singing his praises. There was excellent ale and plenty of fun to be had. The evening wore on, but they continued drinking for a long time. As Hrolf got drunk he began to feel sleepy, so a fine comfortable bed was made ready for him. He threw off his clothes, flung himself on the bed, and instantly fell asleep.

Late that night when Hrolf woke up from an ugly dream, he found himself tied hand-and-foot and shackled securely to a strong beam. He'd been stripped of all his clothes and brought before a great fire. His servant William, the farmer, and the rest of the household were standing over him.

'Now,' said William, 'it's come to this, Hrolf, that I'm in a stronger position than you, and not so long ago you'd hardly have expected that. You've a choice to make. You can burn on this fire and never see the sun again. Or you can accompany me to Russia, serve me in every way, call me your master, and swear to everything I say about myself. You're to perform all my tasks for me, until the King agrees to give me his sister Gyda for a wife, and then you'll be free to leave my service. You're never to take revenge on me for this humiliation, nor on anyone here. Either swear an oath to keep all the conditions I've made, or burn in the fire right now.'

'Since I'm given a chance to get out of your service, I'll agree rather than lose my life,' said Hrolf. 'I know I'll not make much headway with the Earl's mission if I die here. Another thing, I want to stipulate that you never reveal my plans or who I am, otherwise our partnership will be dissolved.'

54

William agreed that. Then Hrolf was set free, and swore an oath according to the custom of the time. So Hrolf became William's servant and pretended not to mind in the least. After that they set out from Olvir's place, with William in the saddle, and Hrolf leading the horse. They travelled through Sweden, and from there to Russia. It's not known which route they followed, but in due course they arrived early in the winter at the town of Ladoga, where King Eirik was in residence. They found themselves lodgings, then set off to present themselves to the King.

CHAPTER 14

Boasting

THIS WAS AT the time of day when the King was at table. They greeted him, and he gave them a friendly reply, asking them who they were.

'I'm called William and this fellow with me is my servant Hrolf,' said William. 'I'm an earl's son from Friesland but I had to make a quick getaway after my own people had tricked me out of my inheritance. I've come here because I've heard all about your splendour and mag-nanimity, and I'd be glad of your hospitality over the winter.'

'I wont begrudge you your food,' said the King. 'I take it you're a great sportsman?'

'I'm master of a good many skills,' said William. 'For one thing, I'm so tough, my strength is inexhaustible. Then I can outrun any animal, quadrupeds and all.'

'A useful talent for thieves,' said the King, 'but one that often comes in handy.'

'I'm not short of talent when it comes to shooting or handling weapons either,' William continued, 'or swimming, or chess, or jousting, or learning and eloquence. If there's anything that lends grace to a man, I've got it.'

'I can see you're not exactly backward in coming forward either,' said the King. 'Now you, Hrolf, tell us what you can do. I've at least as much confidence in him as I have in you, William.'

'There's nothing I can tell you about my talents,' said Hrolf 'because I haven't got any.'

'The skills haven't been fairly shared out,' said the King, 'if one has them all, and the other has none. Take your seats on the lower bench, about half-way down.'

'That's entirely up to you, sir,' said William, 'but I've never been put in such a low seat before.'

They went to their places. Neither Sorkvir nor Brynjolf was at home at that time, as they'd gone north to Giantland with Grim Aegir. William and Hrolf enjoyed every hospitality there, but while William kept tattling on all the time, Hrolf stayed silent and brooding, and took no part in any games with the others. William didn't exactly put his accomplishments on display either. The King was a keen hunter and took great pleasure in deerstalking with his retainers. He'd lived quietly much of the time after coming back to Russia. Everyone was reluctant to attack his Kingdom because of the berserks he had with him, and particularly on account of Grim Aegir's witchcraft and sorcery.

CHAPTER 15

A noble stag

ONE DAY KING Eirik set out into the forest with his retainers, as he often did, to stalk deer and hunt birds. They sighted a stag so fine and big that no one believed he'd ever seen such a magnificent creature before. Most of them agreed that this must be a tame stag, because its horns were incised all over and inlaid with gold, a silver band between, with two gold rings on it. Around its neck was a silver chain, hung with a silver bell which rang out loud whenever the stag ran or even stirred. The King set his mind on catching the stag and told his men to slip the hounds, which they did. The men started to run or ride as fast as they could to capture the stag, but it fled like a mad thing before the hounds, and they could get nowhere near it. They kept after the stag all day but by evening, as dusk began to fall, they had no idea what had become of it. So for three days, that's how it was: they kept sighting the stag but were never able to capture it.

In the evening, the King was back at the drinking table and all his men were seated.

'William,' he said, 'I don't think you're putting on much of a show of your athletic skills. You don't join the others in games or pastimes, and you didn't come into the forest with us.'

'Competing with your men is no pleasure for me, sir,' said William. 'I've seen no one here who's really up to much at sport. Anyway, back home in my own land, I let others go to all the trouble of getting game for the table.'

'We've been chasing a stag for three days, and don't seem to be able to catch it,' said the King. 'If you bring it to us alive with all its trimmings, I'll give you my sister Gyda and power too, for I've never seen anything I want more than that stag. If you're as fleet of foot as you've told us, it should be easy. But you'll have to carry out two more tasks I'll set you. I'll add to your reputation in every possible way and with my support you'll win back all you've lost. If any other man of mine can do this, he'll earn just the same reward for his pains.'

'In the first place, sir,' said William, 'I'm the only one who can do it: and in the second, it happens to be me you've chosen for the job. So I'll either carry it out or die in the attempt.'

They shook hands on agreement, according to custom, but Hrolf paid not the least attention. After that everyone went to bed and took things easy. As usual Hrolf was in constant attendance on William.

Early next morning William and Hrolf got up and set out in search of the stag. They went into the forest and soon saw where the stag was. William started running, as swift as a bird in flight, but the stag simply increased speed. Hrolf lumbered along behind William, who seemed very fast to begin with, and for a long time they raced on and on, with Hrolf always some distance behind. But after a while, William flung himself on the ground and said, 'Anyone who runs himself to death just to get a wife for himself, and money and power, is going to be out of luck.'

Just then Hrolf caught up with William and asked why he was letting the deer get away.

'I could easily keep running,' William answered, 'if I wanted to. But I think that it's your business to capture the stag and carry out all my tasks, if you're man enough to keep your agreement.'

Hrolf didn't say a word, but set off running after the stag, chasing it for a long time until at last he began to catch up with it, for the stag was tiring fast.

Late in the day, they came to a clearing, with a broad, high mound in the middle. The clearing was a lovely sight, with lush grass growing everywhere. As Hrolf was passing the mound, it opened up, so he walked on round it. Then a woman came out, wearing a blue mantle tied with straps, and carrying a light in her hand. 'Not much of a life you're leading, Hrolf,' she said, 'slave to a slave, and now stealing other people's property. The stag you're after is mine, and you'll never catch it unless I let you. But now, come with me into the mound, and then I'll give you a chance to win it. My daughter's in there, and she's under a curse – she can't deliver her child unless a human being lays his hand on her. She's been lying in childbed for nineteen days, and can't give birth. It was I who put the stag under your noses. I knew you'd want to catch it, and would chase it here. I've every faith in your good heart, so come

58

on with me into the mound. But even if someone does bring the stag to the King, he'll never enjoy it.'

'I'll risk going into the mound with you, if it means I can get the stag and bring it to the King, but I don't care what happens to it afterwards,' said Hrolf.

That pleaseed the elfwoman and they went together into the mound. There were splendid rooms inside, very pleasant to look at, but a lot of things there seemed very strange to him. The girl was lying in great agony when he came there, but as soon as Hrolf had laid hands on her, she gave birth to her baby. Both women thanked him with all their hearts and wished him good luck.

'I can't repay you for saving my daughter's life', said the elfwoman, 'but there's a gold ring here I'd like you to have, which you'll find useful when you go to Hreggvid's mound. While you wear it on your finger, you can't lose your way, by day or night, on sea or land, no matter how dark it may be around you. You'll complete all your tasks, but don't ever trust William out of your sight. He'd be glad to see you dead.'

Hrolf thanked her, and then they went outside, where she gave him the stag. Hrolf put it on his back and thought it very handsome. He and the elfwoman said their farewells, and he went on his way. In due course he met William, who was delighted to see him and asked him to carry the stag up to the gate of the town. Hrolf did as he was asked, but he didn't tell William how he'd managed to get the stag. They reached the town late in the evening, when the King was at table.

'Now,' said William, 'we'll go into the hall. I'll carry the stag up to the King, but I want you to back me up so that he'll believe what I tell him.'

The moment William picked up the stag and put it on his back, his knees began to buckle, but he managed to carry it through the hall and up to the King.

He threw it down, huffing and puffing, and said 'Now I think I've earned your sister. Here's the stag: you won't get many brothers-in-law who'll do what I've done.'

'If you ask me, it wasn't you who caught the stag at all,' said the King, 'You'll have to do much more than that before the lady's yours.'

'There's no reason for you to cast doubts on my good name,' said William. 'I'm one of the best men you could get. My servant Hrolf wasn't anywhere near when I caught the stag.'

'I wasn't much use to William,' said Hrolf, 'and he didn't spare himself.'

'The reason why I do everything,' said William, 'is that I want to collect the reward myself. What do you want me to try next, now that I've done this?'

'Go to Hreggvid's burial mound and fetch his armour,' said the King. 'That's no great task.'

'You want to see me dead?' asked William. 'No one who's been there has ever come back alive.'

'I'd be only too pleased if you came back,' said the King. 'But you're right, none of the men I've sent there has ever returned. All the same, I'm very keen to get the armour from the mound; and the man who's going to have my sister has to be the greatest of men.'

'I'll do it,' said William. 'Robbing the dead to win a lady's hand doesn't strike me as difficult.'

Then he went back to his seat, and with that the conversation ended.

CHAPTER 16

To the burial mound

A FEW DAYS went by. Then one night Hrolf tapped William on the leg and said, 'Time to visit the mound and win the lady.'
William got up quickly. Hrolf was already dressed, wearing

Vefreyja's cloak and carrying Atli's spear. William was fully armed. He travelled on horseback, and Hrolf walked ahead. They went on their way till they came to a wood with an old well-trodden path leading through it. When they'd gone a short distance, they ran into rough weather, with so much snow and frost that William couldn't stay in the saddle. Hrolf began leading the horse, with William walking behind for a while, but then the blizzard grew so fierce that the horse couldn't walk, and Hrolf had to drag it along flat on its back behind him, steadying himself with the spear. After a while, glancing back, he saw that William had disappeared and that the horse had been dead for some time so he left it there and walked on. By now the blizzard had reached such a pitch that the trunks of oak trees were snapping off and hurtling through the air. Hrolf got a good many hard knocks which would have killed most men, and but for his cloak, the thunder and lightning would have killed him too. So it went on all night long, till daybreak. Just as day dawned, he was almost bowled over by a terrible stench and had it not been for the cowl on his cloak he'd have suffocated. Hrolf realised that blizzards like this must have killed all the King's messengers, for it was obviously magic weather. He couldn't remember ever having gone through such an ordeal. When it was broad daylight, the weather grew clear and calm, and the stench evaporated. Then Hrolf saw a mound as big as a mountain, surrounded by a high stockade. He took hold of one of the logs of the stockade and swung himself over, but as he climbed up the mound, he realised it was going to be hard to break into.

Looking around, he saw a huge man, regally dressed, standing on the north side of the mound. Hrolf went over, greeted him with the title of King and asked who he was.

'I'm called Hreggvid,' he replied, 'and I dwell in this mound with my champions. You're a welcome visitor, Hrolf. I think you ought to know that I'm responsible for the blizzard, the stench, and the other marvels, but I didn't kill the men. Sorkvir and Grim Aegir are to blame for that; they caused the deaths of the King's messengers, although when there's most at stake, they're not always so clever. If they knew you were here, they'd certainly want you dead. I was the swallow that flew over to Earl Thorgny with a hair of my daughter Ingigerd. I knew that of all the Earl's men only you would search for her, and of all his men you're the one who can save her, as long as your luck holds. I'd rather you married her than any other man, if you're willing to joust against Sorkvir; you're full of courage and strength. Grim Aegir swore to Sorkvir that no one can beat him but the man who wears my armour. That's why the mound was made so hard to break into, with all those barriers in the way. He thought no one could ever get the armour, but I mean to give you anything in the mound that you'd care to take. I'm giving you two sets of armour, very much like one another, but with different properties. Hand the inferior set to the King, but don't let anyone see the other until you use it. Take good care of the sword, because there aren't many like it. My daughter Ingigerd looks after all my tournament weapons and Dulcifal too, that's like almost no other horse. Ride him when you tilt against Sorkvir, and you're sure to win – as long as Dulcifal can be caught. The lance and the shield will still keep their special powers. But once you're free from William's service, don't trust him, because he'll betray you if he can. You'll want to keep your oath; but the sooner he's dead the better, otherwise he'll be a great danger to you.'

Then Hreggvid gave Hrolf the treasures and the weapons. Finally he took the necklace from round his neck and said, 'It's been ordained that I can leave the mound three times, and there's no need to cover it up till after the last time. You won't have any trouble on your way back home. Goodbye now, and may all go as you hope and desire. If you ever come back to Russia, call on me should you need any help.'

At that Hreggvid disappeared into the mound, and Hrolf took over the treasures. He set off from the mound and went back the way he'd come, seeing nothing out of the ordinary. As he left the forest, William

62

came to meet him. He'd crawled under some tree roots and lain there as long as the blizzard lasted, and was so frozen he could hardly speak.

He fawned all over Hrolf and said, 'There aren't words enough to describe what a marvel you are or what luck we're having. Now that the mound's been broken into and the gold and treasures taken from it, I can't see anything to stand in our way. The weather was so foul, I could hardly control my legs, but now I really feel I've won the King's sister, so hand over the treasures and the weapons, I want to present them to the King myself.'

'You aren't doing much to win your own reputation', said Hrolf, 'and though I've risked my life for you, I'll be badly paid for it. But take the treasures and give them to the King; I'll keep my word and back up your story, though you don't deserve it.'

Hrolf had hidden the other set of armour in the wood, so William didn't see it.

They went on their way and in due course found the King sitting at the drinking table after his evening meal. William greeted him and pretended to be worn out. Everyone was amazed to see them back.

'I don't believe there could ever be a worse ordeal than this, all things considered,' said William. 'Hreggvid's such a great troll with all his witchcraft, and the mound was terribly difficult to break into. I spent the whole night battling away with King Hreggvid, and it was touch and go before I could get the armour.'

With that he took the sword and necklace and put them on the table in front of the King.

'Somebody's brought the treasures right enough', said the King, 'though they don't seem to me quite what they used to be, apart from the necklace – that's as good as ever. But I've suspicion that Hrolf must have fetched them.'

'Take my word for it,' said Hrolf, 'I didn't go into the mound; and as you can imagine, I'd hardly deny an achievement like that of my own freewill.'

63

'Sir,' said William, 'I'm amazed that you should cast doubt on my story and suspect my courage and manhood. You can easily test it by letting Hrolf and me try each other's strength. He'll never come up to my standard; to start with, he can't bear the sight of blood. When I went into Hreggvid's mound, he was supposed to hold the rope. But as soon as he heard the banging and clashing in the mound, he got scared and ran away. What saved me was that I'd thrown the end of the rope round a great boulder so I managed to climb up the rope hand over fist.'

'I'll take your word for it, Hrolf,' said the King. 'The treasures wouldn't be here, if no one had fetched them from the mound.'

The King had the armour put into safe keeping, confident that it would cause no trouble to Sorkvir.

The story goes that the stag vanished one night, and those who were guarding it didn't notice. The King missed it badly, and had a thorough search made for it, but it couldn't be found. Hrolf guessed that the elfwoman must have come and taken it. William was very pleased with himself and often went to see the King's sister. They got on well together, and he didn't hesitate to sing his own praises. The winter passed till Christmas, and nothing of importance happened.

CHAPTER 17

Soti

A GREAT AND powerful king called Menelaus ruled over the land of Tartary, believed to be the largest country and the richest in gold throughout the entire Orient. The folk there are big and strong, and the hardest of fighting men. Many tributary kings served under Menelaus, as well as other important chieftains.

It is said that an island lies between Russia and Tartary called Hedin's Isle, an earldom. Learned people say that King Hedin Hjarrandason made this island his first stop when he sailed from India to Denmark, and it has been called after him ever since.[1] The King of Tartary and the King of Russia fought over the island, even though properly it came under the crown of Tartary. King Eirik had raided the island before he came to Russia and had done a great deal of damage there.

King Menelaus had put a man called Soti in charge of the island. His mother's family came from there, but his father's from Novgorod. Soti was away from the island when King Eirik paid his visit. In size and strength, Soti was a real troll, and his complexion suited his name.[2] He attacked many countries and always won. Soti had an old foster-mother, a sorceress, who had once prepared him a bath which made him impregnable to weapons, so he always went into battle without any armour to protect him. She had told him this autumn was the best time to take revenge on King Eirik, as none of his berserks would be at home then. When Soti learned this, he went to see King Menelaus and got a large army from him. Then he set off for Russia with several thousand fighting men. One of them was called Nordri, a big strong man and a great fighter, who used to carry Soti's banner for him.

When King Eirik heard that Soti had arrived in the kingdom with a large force, he had the war-arrow sent out in all directions ordering every able-bodied man to join him, and he mustered a great army. Then he called William before him.

'Now', said the King, 'you've carried out two of the tasks I gave you, though I'm not sure that it was you who performed them. You'll have to carry out your third task, which is to kill the berserk Soti, under my own eyes. If you do this properly, I won't object to your marrying my sister, and I'll keep my agreement with you fully, according to the terms we agreed.'

---

1. This is an allusion to the story of *Hedin and Hogni*, one of the most tragic of the legendary sagas.
2. His name, *Soti*, means "rusty-coloured, dark-brown", or "dark-red".

'I'm quite prepared to meet Soti,' said William. 'I'm glad you recognise now what a remarkable fellow I really am. Choose for me the best weapons there are and the strongest horse you have, and I'll put them to a real test before this battle's over.'

Everything was done just as William had asked, and as usual, Hrolf went along with him on foot. The King travelled with his army until he came face to face with Soti on a level plain with thick woods on one side. There was a great multitude assembled there, as both armies prepared themselves for battle. With horns blaring, the columns began to move against each other, both sides yelling out the war cry.

CHAPTER 18

Single combat

IN THE VAN OF his column, King Eirik marched boldly forward to begin the assault. Soti's men formed up to meet him, and fierce fighting broke out, with both sides thrusting forward.

Once the fighting started, William rode off into a clearing in the wood. 'Now, William,' said Hrolf, 'it's time for you to go ahead, kill Soti, and win the lady's hand.'

'I may win myself a wife and a kingdom, if that's what fate has in store for me,' said William, 'but I'll never try to earn them by risking my life in battle. What's the good of wife and kingdom if I lose my own life? If you want to free yourself from your bondage and slavery take my weapons and horse, ride ahead and kill Soti, otherwise you'll find yourself in my service for the rest of your days.'

Hrolf took the horse and William's weapons, and rode over to the battlefield. It had been a deadly struggle, and King Eirik was losing ground fast under the Tartars' fierce attack. Soti and Nordri pushed forward resolutely and destroyed everything in their path. Soti fought

66

with a halberd, hacking and thrusting over and over again. Nordri carried his fine sword boldly forward. King Eirik had forced his way into the thick of Soti's troops, till Nordri came against him with a crowd of Tartars. They attacked the King fiercely, and many of his troops were cut down, so that he found himself sorely pressed by the enemy. Then Hrolf charged so fiercely with William's weapons that Soti's troops were forced back, as he struck and lunged to right and left, killing man after man until he reached King Eirik. In this attack, Hrolf killed more than thirty men.

When Soti saw this he turned in a rage to meet Hrolf and lunged at him with the halberd. Hrolf warded off the blow with his shield, and thrust at Soti's chest, but the spear didn't bite and broke at the socket. Grasping his sword with both hands, Soti swung at Hrolf. The stroke fell on the middle of Hrolf's shield, slicing it in two, and cleaving through the horse as well, just in front of the forelegs so that the sword stuck in the ground. This left Hrolf standing on his own two feet, exhausted by a whole day of battle. While King Eirik continued his fierce encounter with Nordri, Hrolf sliced the head off Soti's horse, so that now both men were fighting on foot. Soti struck at Hrolf, but he dodged the blow, and the halberd plunged deep into the earth right up to Soti's hands. Hrolf crashed his sword two-handed so hard down on Soti's shoulder that it broke off at the hilt. In a fury, Hrolf rushed up to Soti and drove the pointed hilt into his head, right into the brain. There was nothing he could do about it, and he fell to the ground, dead. By then King Eirik had killed Nordri, and every single Tartar began to run off as fast as he could. King Eirik and his men routed them, killing everyone they laid hands on. They gained a great deal of plunder there, gold and silver, weapons, clothes, and other precious things as well.

Hrolf took no part in the chase. He got himself a horse, vaulted into the saddle, and rode into the wood to give William news of what had happened. Hrolf told him to take the horse and his weapons: 'Put on a bold face,' he said, 'and get things ready for the wedding feast.'

'It's a brave battle we've fought,' said William. 'I must be a man of great wit and wisdom to have achieved so much. One of these days I'll be famous.' Hrolf smiled at his words and said William wasn't doing much to earn his fame for himself.

William mounted the horse, and rode with full harness over to Gyda, the King's sister, to boast about his bravery and warlike deeds. King Eirik was already home and had started drinking in his hall.

William went up to greet the King.

'It was a close thing for you today before I came to your rescue, sir,' he said. 'You've no reason to doubt me and my deeds any longer; nothing is too much for me.'

'I think, William,' said the King, 'that the weapons and armour were yours, but the hands were Hrolf's'.

'There's nothing I'd like better,' said Hrolf, 'than to have the right to claim all William's valiant deeds as my own, but I shan't go far by stealing honours that are not mine and that I was never born to win.'

'It will seem very strange, sir, to all who hear about it', said William, 'the way you keep casting doubt on my great deeds and distinctions. Do you think it more suitable for a peasant lad to achieve all this and win your sister? Because that's all Hrolf is, and people won't consider him the likeliest of chieftains to rule over them and perform heroic deeds. Now, I am an earl in my own right, son of an earl and of royal stock. I'm handsome and brave, a remarkable man in every way, with all the qualities suited to a nobleman. If you refuse me the betrothal and marriage we'd agreed upon, I'll go about spreading your shame in every land, how you've cheated me and broken your word and your faith. Back home where I live, everyone would agree that any princess who married me would think it a great honour'.

'I don't want it put about that I've cheated you,' said King Eirik. 'I'll keep my part of our bargain, but somehow I can't get Hrolf out of my mind. I just don't see what it is the two of you are up to. Things aren't as they seem.'

With that their conversation ended, and the King began to prepare for the wedding. There was a splendid banquet during which William married King Eirik's sister Gyda, without any objection on her part. William had a swarm of servants in attendance on him, and was full of his own importance.

CHAPTER 19

Freedom

EARLY ONE MORNING Hrolf walked into the room where William was sleeping and went up to the bed. 'It's come to this, William,' he said, 'I've been your servant, and now at last you're the King's brother-in-law, so I'm resigning from your service, and our agreement's come to an end. You can be quite easy in your mind about our parting. I'm more concerned with my own honour than with your deserts.'

With that Hrolf went off, leaving William completely flabbergasted. Gyda asked why Hrolf had left so suddenly, and why he'd spoken like that.

'He never wants to be more than a month or two in the same place if he can help it,' said William, 'it's simply the way he's made, and I've had to frighten him into staying on here since I came. There's proof positive that anyone who gives him a job is going to regret it. Hrolf's wicked through and through, a thief and a villian. I don't want the responsibility of having him put to death in a foreign country; but he'll soon show what sort of stuff he's made of. No matter what anyone does to help him, he pays them back with trouble.'

With that they dropped the subject, and the wedding feast continued in grand style.

The story goes that after all the losses they'd suffered, the remnants of

Soti's troops sailed back to Tartary. King Menelaus thought their trip had been a sorry business, but there was nothing he could do about it.

Early in the Spring Sorkvir and Brynjolf came back from Giantland bringing Eirik many of the most rare treasures. With Grim Aegir's help they'd won all the battles they'd fought. Hrolf stayed on at the royal court, on bad terms with Sorkvir, Brynjolf, and William, but very friendly with his neighbours: and though he'd never done anyone a good turn while he was in William's service, now he was always handing out silver.

This was the third year the Princess was supposed to find a man to joust against Sorkvir, and as King Eirik didn't think it likely she could find anyone, he was very pleased with himself.

CHAPTER 20
A tilter chosen

SHORTLY AFTERWARDS MESSENGERS came to King Eirik from the Princess, and asked him to call people to a large assembly where she would choose a man to joust against Sorkvir, saying that if she failed to find anyone, she would be ready to join the King according to their agreed settlement. This message delighted the King. He felt he'd as good as won the Princess, and just as she had called together all the most powerful people from her part of the kingdom, he too summoned a great assembly from towns and castles and all the neighbouring districts. A good many uninvited guests came as well, for most of the people were curious to see how things would turn out, and all of them were deeply concerned for her.

The assembly was held a short distance from Princess Ingigerd's castle. King Eirik came to the meeting with a large following, including Sorkvir, Brynjolf, and his brother-in-law William. Hrolf was there too, carrying Hreggvid's weapons, but no one paid any attention to him. A huge crowd had already gathered, and this is how people sat: the seats were arranged in circles with one gangway for people to go through; William was seated next to the King, with Sorkvir and Brynjolf immediately below him, but the King's other followers were placed elsewhere. Hrolf was placed low in the outer circle on a very humble seat.

After everything had been arranged, Princess Ingigerd arrived at the assembly, so lovely and desirable that no one could praise her beauty too much. Everyone except Hrolf gazed at her, but he didn't even throw a glance in her direction, and kept the hood pulled down over his face. The Princess came up to every man and looked into his eyes; she walked round the first circle, then the next. Eventually she came to Hrolf, and took him by the hand, but he didn't move from his seat. Then she pushed back his hood.

'There's not much of a choice of men here,' she said, 'but this is the one I choose to joust against Sorkvir on my behalf. So, if he's willing, he must come with me.'

'You've made a very unwise choice,' said Hrolf. 'I can't even ride without help and keep falling off, and I'm easily scared, even when people just make faces at me.'

'I've never seen you before,' said the Princess: 'but you won't get out of this, not if I can help it.'

'My lady,' said King Eirik, 'I thought you were supposed to choose a man from this country, not a foreigner. Hrolf is William's servant and one of my men, so he's free to refuse.'

'Here in Russia I'm nobody's servant', said Hrolf, 'and if it will help the Princess to her freedom, I'll gladly grant her first request to me.'

Then Hrolf rose to his feet and went over to the castle with the Princess and her retinue. She seated Hrolf on the throne and did everything she could to honour and entertain him.

After King Eirik left the assembly, he went gloomily to another

71

castle. Everybody was surprised that the Princess had chosen the man who seemed least likely to win, but the King bitterly regretted his promise to the Princess. He urged Sorkvir to do all he could, and not spare any trick he might have up his sleeve.

'This man has always been something of a worry to me', he said, 'but take good care of Hreggvid's armour, and he won't be able to hurt us.'

Hrolf remained in the castle with the Princess, enjoying the best of entertainment. He told her about his mission on the Earl's behalf, and she said she knew all about that.

'I want to go away from here with you,' she said. 'If you get me out of the hands of my enemies, you're the one who'll most deserve me.' And that was the end of their conversation.

Next morning Hrolf got up early, and put on Hreggvid's armour, with the fine sword at his side. The Princess gave him the shield and lance her father used to carry, then told him to go and catch the horse Dulcifal. He was driven into a strong corral with lot of other horses, where he kept biting and kicking, killing a number of them, but when Hrolf went up to the corral and struck the lance against the shield, Dulcifal walked right up to him; and the shield and lance rang out so loudly, everyone there was amazed. Hrolf took hold of the horse, saddled him, and vaulted neatly onto his back wearing full armour, whereupon Dulcifal sprang forward, cleared the bars comfortably, and charged into the lists. Sorkvir was already there, along with the King, William, Brynjolf, and a host of people.

CHAPTER 21

Tournament

BOTH CONTESTANTS AIMED their lances ready for the attack, and charged one another as hard as their horses could go. As they clashed, Sorkvir's lance struck Hrolf's shield, but glanced aside, whereas Hrolf knocked off Sorkvir's helm. By the time that Hrolf had completed the charge, Sorkvir had only covered two thirds of the course. Dulcifal turned back, refusing to stop, and Sorkvir hadn't covered more than a quarter of the field when they clashed again. Each struck at the other, but just as before, Sorkvir made no headway, this time losing his shield. In the third charge, Dulcifal went as swift as a bird in flight, and again they clashed. Hrolf thrust at Sorkvir, and his spear caught in the mailcoat. He heaved Sorkvir right out of the saddle, rode with him across the field, and threw him into a stinking pit, breaking his neck. Dulcifal stood as quiet as if he were anchored to the earth.

The Princess and all her people were overjoyed, but when King Eirik saw this, he flew into a rage, ordering his men to surround Hrolf and kill him on the spot. He said that if Hrolf got away with it this time there'd be no end to the trouble he'd cause. As the King had ordered them, his men attacked Hrolf on all sides. When Dulcifal saw this he reared up, striking out with his front legs, and biting a good many of them to death. His eyes were like balls of blood, and fires seemed ablaze in his mouth and nostrils. He galloped forward, trampling on everyone in his way. Nor was Hrolf wasting his time in the saddle. He was testing Hreggvid's sword, hewing and thrusting right and left at men and horses, so that all in his path were doomed. The troops fell back, and Hrolf rode towards the King, but Eirik saved himself by running away.

Hrolf killed more than a hundred men before he reached the forest, exhausted but completely unhurt. But as King Eirik saw it, he'd suffered enormous losses in men and when he went back home in the evening to his castle he was very glum indeed.

That evening the Princess gave all her men plenty to drink, and conducted herself very cheerfully. She got all her ladies-in-waiting so drunk they dropped off to sleep on the spot. Early during the night Hrolf came back to the castle, found the Princess, and told her to prepare for a journey with him. She said she was quite ready. Hrolf had two big coffers with him for her jewels. Then they both mounted Dulcifal and rode on their way. The story doesn't tell us which route they took or how long they travelled, but they went more by night than by day.

CHAPTER 22

William's vow

NOW WE COME back to King Eirik. When he woke up in the morning, he told his men to arm themselves and try to find Hrolf. They did as they were told, and searched for three days without seeing any sign of him. Then the King ordered a search of the Princess' castle, but she'd already left, and no one knew what had happened to her. This made the King thoroughly scared and all the more angry.

'I can see you've been telling me a pack of lies about yourself and Hrolf,' he said to William. 'It's only too obvious that he's not the man you said he was. I realise now, it must have been Hrolf who went into the mound, not you. That's how he got the good suit of armour, and I got the useless one. Anybody could see he was of noble birth; and, as for you, you're a spineless traitor and a coward throughout every fibre of your body! You must have known everything about his plans and were too frightened to tell me anything. For one thing, I think you have no kingdom, nor anything else to your credit; and, for another, I'm convinced you're no more than a slave and a bumpkin. I ought to give you what you really deserve, and hang you on a gallows, for all your lies and treachery to my sister and myself. That's how you'll end up one day, even if it doesn't happen just yet.'

By the time the King had finished speaking, William was frightened out of his wits. 'Yet again I'll show you what sort of man I am,' he said. 'Standing on this log, I make a solemn vow never to get into Gyda's bed until I've killed Hrolf and brought you his head and the Princess. I'll do this without the strength and assistance of any other man.'

William took his weapons and horse and rode off as fast as he could in search of Hrolf, but King Eirik stayed behind in Russia and wasn't at all pleased with the way things were going.

CHAPTER 23

The dwarf

THE STORY NOW shifts to Earl Thorgny and his troops in Denmark. In the autumn when Hrolf left for Russia, the Earl set out on his usual tour of the Kingdom.

One day a stranger calling himself Mondul Pattason, appeared before the Earl. He said he'd travelled widely in foreign parts and had plenty to tell the Earl, as he'd performed many a brave deed. He was very short, but sturdily built, with a handsome face, and bulging eyes. The Earl gave this man a friendly welcome and an invitation to stay, which Mondul accepted. He would often amuse the Earl with his many entertaining stories. In time the Earl started treating him as a close friend and consulted him on all his problems. Mondul would sit talking with him day and night, so that the Earl began to neglect matters of state.

One day Bjorn the Counsellor came to the Earl, as he often did, to complain about his taking a stranger into his confidence, particularly since their consultations had gone so far that the Earl no longer paid proper attention to affairs of state. The Earl grew angry at Bjorn's criticism and said that whatever Bjorn might say, he'd do just as he pleased. Mondul heard Bjorn's words, but said nothing himself. Bjorn told the Earl a few home truths before he left.

Bjorn had a town house by the Earl's residence, and a mansion in the country too, as we've already said. One day when Bjorn was out, Mondul came to his house. There was no one at home except Ingibjorg, Bjorn's wife, and he started flirting with her, but she took it in good part. In the end he asked her to sleep with him, tempting her with a great deal of sweet talk. He offered her a lot of valuable gifts and with every word he belittled Bjorn, saying he wasn't a real man.

Ingibjorg got very angry at this and answered him very contemptuously, saying she'd never go with him. Then Mondul brought out a jug from under his cloak and asked her to drink to their reconciliation, but she knocked the jug from beneath with her hand, splashing all its contents into his face. Mondul was furious.

'I shan't be finished with you or your husband Bjorn,' he said, 'until I've paid you back for all you've done and said to shame me.'

He went away and presented himself to Earl Thorgny. 'Sir,' he said, 'I'd take it as a great courtesy if you'd accept this belt I inherited from my father.' And he placed it on the table in front of the Earl. It was set with precious jewels and ornamented all over with gold. The Earl thought he'd never seen a gift of such value. He thanked Mondul, adding that he'd never received a gift like it from a commoner. Mondul stayed over winter enjoying the same favours, but Stefnir and Bjorn weren't at all fond of him. The Earl was very pleased with the belt, and at every feast he held, he would show it to his friends.

That winter Ingibjorg, Bjorn's wife, caught some strange illness. She grew black as death and paid no attention to anything, just as though she'd gone insane. Bjorn was deeply distressed, for he loved her dearly.

In the spring, at some feast or other, Mondul's belt vanished suddenly from the Earl's keeping. They looked for it everywhere, but it couldn't be found. The Earl reckoned it a great loss and insisted that they should make a more thorough search for it, but still it couldn't be found. The Earl asked Mondul what he thought could have happened to it, and where they should look.

'It would be a tricky business to point the finger at the man who took it,' said Mondul, 'though I can make a shrewd guess at who he is. And it's likely that the man who's taken the belt will have stolen more from you than just this one thing. Whoever did this must be a man of importance, someone who's always been jealous of your high rank. Now, it's my advice that you mount a thorough search. Start with those who're above suspicion and don't exclude anyone, no matter how notable he may be. A man like the one who's stolen the belt will never open his coffers of his own free will. And whoever's guilty must be hanged on the gallows.'

The Earl thought this a good idea and ordered it to be carried out. He called all his retainers together and told them he wanted to search everyone's coffers, first his son Stefnir's, then Bjorn the Counsellor's, so that others would all the more readily accept. They said they were quite willing. First Stefnir opened his coffers, and nothing was found in them. Next a search was made at Bjorn's, and in the houses of other retainers in town, but nothing was found there, either.

Then Mondul said, 'Bjorn must have other coffers, apart from those in his town house, and they've not been searched.'

'Bjorn has some out of town, true enough,' said Stefnir, 'but I'm sure there's no point in searching them.'

All the same, the Earl insisted on going there, and that's what they did. Bjorn agreed to a house search, just as before. Mondul went up to an old chest and asked what it contained. Bjorn said nothing but old boat nails. The Earl ordered him to open the chest: but when Bjorn looked for the key, he couldn't find it. Then the Earl broke open the chest, emptying out all its contents, and there lying at the bottom was the belt. Everyone was flabbergasted, Bjorn most of all, because he knew himself to be innocent.

In a rage, the Earl ordered Bjorn's arrest. 'I'll have you hanged on the highest gallows as soon as it's daylight,' he said. 'He must have done this sort of thing before, though it's only now that he's been found out.'

They seized Bjorn and tied him up securely, and though everyone knew he didn't deserve this treatment, nobody dared raise any objection. Bjorn offered to submit himself to an ordeal, according to custom, but the Earl wouldn't hear of it. Stefnir managed to extract one favour from his father, that Bjorn wasn't to be killed for seven days, in case anything turned up to prove his innocence. He was to be placed in Mondul's custody and not allowed into town. Plenty of people were unhappy about all this, as Bjorn was a very popular man. The Earl went back home to town with his men, and they all started drinking. No sooner had the retainers tasted the first course and drunk the first glass than all their friendship for Bjorn evaporated, and everybody agreed that he must be guilty.

Mondul remained on Bjorn's estate and drove all his household away. He took Ingibjorg to bed every night, before Bjorn's very eyes, and she showed Mondul every affection, not even remembering her husband Bjorn. He found it hard to bear, but that was how the seven days we've mentioned went by.

Now the story returns to the point where we left it, for it's not possible to tell two stories at the very same time, even though that may have been the way they happened.

CHAPTER 24

William again

IT'S TIME NOW to return to Hrolf and the Princess, who were travelling from Russia. One day they saw someone come riding after them in linen drawers, with a sword at his side. Soon he caught up with them, and Hrolf recognised William. When he came up to Hrolf, he threw himself down at his feet and begged for mercy in every possible way. 'I've suffered terribly since we parted,' said William. 'The King had me thrown into a dungeon and even wanted me killed; but starving and frozen stiff as I was, my cunning saw me through. Now I'm at your mercy, dear Hrolf, you can do just what you like with me but I promise never to do anything to upset you again, and I'll be loyal and faithful to you for ever, as long as you spare my life and let me go back to Denmark with you.'

Hrolf was touched by William's lament. He said he wouldn't go to the trouble of killing him, even though he deserved it. The Princess said Hrolf was making a big mistake. 'He's got a nasty look about him,' she said, 'and he'll turn out to be a bad lot.'

William travelled with them and put on an appearance of servility, but he could never come anywhere near Dulcifal, for the horse would bite and kick him whenever he got the chance.

They kept going till they were within a day's journey of Earl Thorgny's residence, then stopped overnight in a certain wood, building themselves a shelter of branches in the evening. At night, Hrolf and the Princess would lie side by side, with a naked sword between them. During the night William stuck a sleep-thorn into Hrolf, and early in the morning he got up, fetched the horse Dulcifal and saddled him, this being the only thing the horse would let William do for him. Hrolf slept in his armour, with Vefreyja's cloak on top. Ingigered got up and tried hard to rouse Hrolf but couldn't wake him, no matter how much she tried. She left the shelter and burst into tears. When William saw this, he asked didn't she enjoy sleeping with Hrolf?

'I like everything about him,' she said, 'but he's sleeping so fast that I can't wake him up.'

'I'll wake him,' said William.

Going to the shelter, he tore it apart and cut off both of Hrolf's feet, then hid them under his coat. Hrolf slept on undisturbed. The Princess asked what was it she'd heard break?

'Hrolf's lifespan,' said William.'

'A curse on your life and on the hand that did this,' said the Princess, 'it's the vilest of things that you've done, and an evil end that's coming to you.'

'I'll offer you a choice,' said William; 'and you can take your pick. I don't think there's any honour in it for me to go back to Russia; so you can come with me to Earl Thorgny and back up everything I say, or I can kill you here and now.'

She thought she'd better not choose death as long as she had a chance, but it seemed to her that nothing was too underhand for William. She told him she'd go along with him and back him up, as long as he said nothing to dishonour her, and to this he forced her to swear an oath. William wanted to get hold of Dulcifal, but there was no chance of that now as the horse was biting and kicking in all directions, and William couldn't get anywhere near him, nor would the horse let him near Hrolf either. As for the sword, it was far too heavy for William to carry. So Hrolf was left lying there as the other two went on their way, but the Princess was heartbroken at having to leave him there in such a state.

There's nothing to tell of their journey till they reached Earl Thorgny, who came out to welcome the Princess with all honour and joy. He asked William who he was.

'I'm a farmer's son of good Danish stock,' said William, 'and joined up with Hrolf on his way to Russia. We performed a good many great deeds there, but when Hrolf beat and killed King Eirik's champion, Sorkvir, that was his last triumph. The King wouldn't stand for it and had Hrolf arrested and put to death. I've got his feet here with me to show you. After that I rescued the Princess and brought her here with me. Many's the time I risked my life for your sake, and so did Hrolf. There wasn't a braver man, and he didn't give up till he'd lost both his legs. And now I think I've earned your daughter Thora for my wife. You needn't be ashamed of having me for a son-in-law, considering my background and bravery. There's no need to put off our two weddings, we could celebrate them both at the same time.'

Most people thought William's story likely enough, and everyone was saddened by Hrolf's death, particularly the Earl and his son, Stefnir. Ingigerd wept bitterly; and in comforting her, the Earl asked whether William had been telling her the truth.

'William's not likely to tell you more lies than he tells others,' she said. 'But I'd like to ask you the favour of postponing the weddings for a month. Plenty may happen in the meantime to make you change your mind.'

Thora didn't like the look of William, either, and asked for the same delay. When William heard about this he began to bluster. 'Whatever they say, you mustn't postpone the wedding,' he said. 'No notice should ever be taken of women's whims.'

'It's right and proper that the Princess should have her way in this' said Stefnir. 'The delay isn't a long one.'

'That's not the behaviour of a chieftain,' said William, 'letting women make his decisions and change his plans – or a son either, when he gives bad advice.'

Stefnir grew angry at William's words. 'The ladies,' he said, 'not William, shall have their way, even if I die for it.'

William said it would be no loss if Stefnir were to be killed. The Earl told them not to let this business cause a quarrel between them.

'Stefnir had better have his way now he's decided to meddle in it,' said the Earl, 'but you'll get my daughter in marriage, William, you deserve her.'

Taking Ingigerd by the hand, Stefnir led her to his sister's boudoir, where he locked her up and kept the key himself. It's said that Ingigerd preserved Hrolf's feet by applying certain herbs to them which prevented them from dying. William didn't like Stefnir at all, but there was nothing he could do about it.

CHAPTER 25

Recovery

NOW WE RETURN to Hrolf. He lay till evening like a dead man, as the sleep-thorn was still stuck in his head – William hadn't taken it out. Saddled and bridled, Dulcifal kept watch over him. Then the horse moved closer and started rolling Hrolf about with his head, whereupon the sleep-thorn fell out. So Hrolf woke up to find both his feet missing, no sign of the shelter, and William vanished with the Princess. The sword that had once been Hreggvid's was still lying there. Hrolf thought things weren't looking too good for him, but he stirred himself, got hold of the healing stones, and began rubbing the stumps of his legs. Soon all the pain had gone from the wounds. Hrolf crawled to the horse, and Dulcifal lay down so that Hrolf could roll himself into the saddle. Then Dulcifal stood up, and Hrolf rode on his way till he came to the mansion of his friend Bjorn – he didn't want to ride into town, and his own castle seemed too far off. After Hrolf had ridden into the garden, Dulcifal lay down. Hrolf took the bridle off the horse and crawled into the house. Everything there seemed to him very luxurious.

Hrolf entered the main hall and threw himself down onto a seat in the shadows, where he lay for some time. Then he saw a woman moving about, carrying fire. She was dark-skinned and wearing dark clothes, and she was swollen all over. The woman lit the fire. Shortly afterwards a man entered the hall, short and broad in the waistline, wearing scarlet clothes, a golden fillet round his hair, and leading someone behind him, chained hand and foot. Hrolf recognised his friend Bjorn, and from what he could see, Bjorn was being given a hard time. The man pushed Bjorn aside, sat down by the fire, lifted the woman onto his knee and started kissing her.

'That's a wicked thing, Mondul,' said Bjorn. 'You seduce my wife and slander me before the Earl with all those lies, so that he's going to hang me in three days for no reason at all. This could never have happened had Hrolf Sturlaugsson been here, and if he's destined to return, he'll avenge me.'

'He'll neither help you nor avenge you,' answered Mondul. 'I can tell you something – both his feet have been cut off, and he's as good as dead. He'll never get back alive.'

Hrolf stood up on the stumps of his legs, and grabbed Mondul's throat with both hands. 'And I can tell you something,' he said; 'Hrolf's hands are still alive, even though his feet are gone.' Then he forced Mondul down under him till he gurgled.

'Please don't kill me, Hrolf,' said Mondul. 'I swear I'll heal you, I've the finest ointment in the whole of Scandinavia. I'm so clever at medicine that if anyone has the least chance of survival, I can cure him in only three days. I'd better explain, too, that I'm a dwarf, an earth-dweller, and I possess the dwarf's magical skills both as healer and smith. I came here because I wanted to bewitch Thora, the Earl's daughter, or Ingibjorg, and take one of them away with me. But since Bjorn understood better than anyone else what I'm really like, I wanted to destroy him. I took the belt and put it in his chest, and then hid the key to it, because the slower he was to open the chest, the more likely he'd seem to have stolen the belt. I've turned every man's friendship away from Bjorn. Now I want to save my own life. I'll do anything you want, and I'll never betray the man who spares me.'

'I'll take the risk and spare your life,' Hrolf said. 'But, first of all, you have to cure Ingibjorg and set Bjorn free.'

He let Mondul stand up, just as dark and ugly as he'd been created. Mondul untied Bjorn, then he undressed Ingibjorg, rubbed her skin with some fine ointment, and gave her a drink to bring back her memory. She soon came to her senses, whereupon her skin became white again, her good health was restored, and she lost her love for the dwarf. She and Bjorn thanked Hrolf, as indeed he deserved.

After that Mondul disappeared, and came back a while later, carrying Hrolf's feet and a huge jar of ointment. 'Now I'm going to do something I'd never planned, Hrolf,' he said, 'and that's to heal you. Just lie down by the fire, and warm the stumps.'

So that's what Hrolf did. Then the dwarf applied the ointment to the wounds, placed the feet against them, and bound them with splints. He had Hrolf lie in bed for three days, and after that he removed the dressing and told Hrolf to get up and try his strength. That's what Hrolf did, and the feet were just as relaxed and supple as if he'd never been wounded.

Now even if people think such a thing incredible, it's still everyone's responsibility to say whatever he's seen or heard. And it isn't easy to contradict what has been said in the past by men of learning. Had they wished, they could surely have told a very different tale if it had happened any other way. Then there are wise men who have written figuratively – men such as Master Gualterus in *Alexander's Saga* and the poet Homer in *Trójumanna Saga*.[1] Masters who have come after these

---

1. *Alexander's Saga* is the Icelandic version (made by Brand Jonsson *c.* 1260) of the Latin *Alexandreis* of Philippus Gualterus de Castilione. (Phillipe Gautier de Chatillon). *Trójumanna Saga* ('The Saga of the Men of Troy') is derived from the Latin of Dares Phrygius and Dictys Cretensis.

have vouched for the truth of what was written, and not denied that things might have happened that way. No one however need take it as literal truth when he can just listen to the story and enjoy himself.

Then Hrolf said to Mondul, 'You've done well to heal me, and I'll do you any favour you care to ask. Another thing, I'd like you to come with me to Russia if I go back there.'

Mondul agreed to do so – 'but now,' he added, 'I want to go back to my own place. I've had the worst of it in our dealings, and the greatest blow of all was to lose Ingibjorg. But that's the way it has to be.'

With that Mondul left, and what happened to him next Hrolf had no idea.

CHAPTER 26

Reunion

NEXT MORNING HROLF got up and put on his armour. 'Now we'd better go to town and see the Earl,' he said.

'I'm not keen to do that,' said Bjorn; 'the seven days' grace I was given is over now, and it's certain death for me if I go back there.'

'That's a risk you'll have to take,' said Hrolf.

So they went to the town and walked into the hall, stopping just inside the door. The Earl was sitting at table drinking, but neither he nor anyone else in the hall recognised Hrolf. However, as soon as the Earl's retainers saw Bjorn they all began to talk.

'That thief Bjorn's getting very bold,' they said, 'coming before the Earl like this. Mondul can't have been guarding him properly – he must have escaped.'

One of the retainers picked up the huge joint bone of an ox and flung it at Bjorn, but Hrolf took it in flight and hurled it back at the man who'd thrown it. The bone caught him in the chest, went right through him, and stuck fast in the wooden wall behind. Everyone was shaken by this and terrified by the big man who'd suddenly appeared.

Hrolf said to Bjorn, 'Walk up to Stefnir's seat and say this to him: 'Hrolf Sturlaugsson would invite you in, if he were in your place, and you were the visitor'.

In a state of terror, Bjorn sidled slowly up the hall till he reached Stefnir, then he repeated Hrolf's words. As soon as Stefnir heard them, he vaulted over the table, walked down to where Hrolf was, and lifted the hood from his face. He recognised Hrolf, welcomed him warmly and led him up to his father. The Earl was delighted to see that Hrolf had returned and stood up to embrace him.

When he saw Hrolf, William didn't know where to turn his eyes. One moment he was red in the face, and the next as white as lime bark with fear.

'It looks to me as if Hrolf's here, William,' said Earl Thorgny, 'and not dead at all.'

Hrolf asked where William was.

'Here I am, dear Hrolf,' he said, 'entirely at your mercy.'

'That wasn't a very friendly leave you took of me, William,' said Hrolf. 'These ugly memories must have been squatting in your heart for a very long time, though now they're coming to light. You'd better tell us the story of your past life, ugly as it is, because there's not much of a life ahead of you.'

'Just as you wish, dear Hrolf,' said William, 'that would be the best thing to do.'

CHAPTER 27

William's story

'**M**Y STORY STARTS like this. Ulf, my father, worked a farm on the edge of a forest here in Denmark. He was married with eight children, the oldest being myself. My father had a good many goats, very tricky to herd, and I had the job of looking after them. In fact I had to do every kind of job that came to hand if I could, but my clothes were poor, and I had scarcely a thing to eat. If I didn't get the goats home, I was beaten. I found it a hard life to put up with, so one night, when I got home, I set fire to the house and burned the lot of them to death inside. After that I stayed on the farm for quite some time till I was a bit stronger.

'One night I dreamt a huge man came to me calling himself Grim. He told me I showed a lot of promise and that as long as I was ready to go out and seek it, I had a great future. Then he asked me to strike a bargain with him, and I asked what sort of bargain.

'I'll give you more strength than you've ever had before,' said Grim 'as well as weapons and fine clothes and lots of other things; and in return you're to go and find Hrolf Sturlaugsson and try to kill him. He's just on his way to Russia and means to run off with the Princess. If he's not done away with, he'll cause no end of trouble. Maybe we'll be able to change your luck so that he'll be killed and you'll become King Eirik's brother-in-law.'

'After I agreed, he took a horn from under his cloak and gave me a drink from it, and I seemed to feel power surging up in me. So we parted, and when I woke, I saw the weapons and the clothes lying there. Then I set off, and in due course the two of us met my kinsman Olvir. Everything that happened there was my idea, as I felt sure you'd never break your oath, Hrolf, and that later on I'd get the chance to kill you, in my own time, once you'd helped me to achieve what I wanted. Now I see that it must have been Grim Aegir who appeared to me, and that's why I left Russia. I was afraid he'd take it out on me for not doing what he'd told me to. I'd made up my mind to get Thora for a wife, and that's why I brought Ingigerd here, not to Russia. I'd never have been safe there if the truth about myself had come out. I planned to kill Stefnir, then the Earl and after that I'd have taken Ingigerd and become sole ruler of the country. I'd have killed you there and then in the wood, dear Hrolf, if I hadn't been so scared of Dulcifal. And that's the end of my life story. I hope you'll let me live, dear Hrolf, though I don't deserve it. There was some excuse for me; I wanted every scrap of honour I could get. What a marriage, and what a kingdom!'

William said no more, but everyone there who'd heard the story thought him the most miserable of traitors.

Then Hrolf started to tell his story, beginning with the time he set off from Denmark right up to the present. Everyone was very impressed with his reputation and exploits, and thought the dwarf must have been sent to save him.

Bjorn was given back all the honours and rank he'd enjoyed before, and William was taken prisoner. Then people were summoned to a great assembly, where they determined what kind of death he should suffer. All agreed it ought to be the most fearful end, so a stick was put between his jaws, and he was hanged on the highest gallows. That, in so many words, was the death of William, and it was no more than was to be expected that such a vile man should come to a vile end, traitor and murderer that he was.

Princess Ingigerd was very happy now that Hrolf had come back safe and well. The Earl had a talk with her and told her there was no need to put off the wedding any longer.

'May I remind you, sir,' she said, 'that King Hreggvid, my father, hasn't been avenged yet, and that I'll not go into any man's bed until that's been done, and King Eirik is dead, along with Grim Aegir and all the others most to blame. Nor will I have Russia ruled by any man but the one I'm going to marry.'

'Since I was the one who rescued the Princess from Russia,' said Hrolf, 'and since she was happy enough to come with me, she's not going to be forced to do anything against her own will if I can help it. But I'd like to make you an offer, sir, to go with your troops to Russia and accomplish all I can there.'

'Thank you for your goodwill,' said the Earl, 'in this and in everything else you've done for me. I'd very much like you and Stefnir to lead this expedition. I'll fit you out with all the ships and men I can afford, and then I want you to take whatever vengeance the Princess desires. The wedding won't take place until, destiny willing, you return.'

The Princess said she was very satisfied with this, so it was agreed on. Hrolf's men had been waiting for him in the castle all the time he was away, and they were happy to have him back.

CHAPTER 28

Back to Russia

DURING THE SUMMER Earl Thorgny had ships built and weapons forged, and gathered them in from every part of his kingdom. He also had with him a lot of men from Sweden and Friesland, sent by his friends and kinsmen, and some from Wendland, too. In Jutland, great preparations for this expedition were under way, and by the time the whole army had been assembled they had a fine, well-equipped force, with a hundred ships, mostly big ones. Hrolf and Stefnir, the leaders of the force, delayed for some days waiting for favourable winds.

89

One day a man came up to Hrolf's ship. He was short and sturdily built, and carried a big bundle on his back. As he came up the gangway, Hrolf recognised him as Mondul, the dwarf, and gave him a friendly welcome.

Mondul put down the bundle and said, 'Well, here I am, Hrolf, just as you asked, and I'll go with you, if that's what you want, on condition that I'm put in charge whenever I choose, and no one disobeys my orders. We'll have to put everything we've got into it, if we're going to succeed.'

Hrolf said that everyone would follow Mondul's advice, and that he was glad to have the dwarf with him.

Then the dwarf said, 'Here's my first order, Hrolf: you're to be on the leading ship throughout the voyage. You have the ring the elfwoman gave you, so you won't lose your way. We're to link all the ships together, each one to the prow of the next, and I'll be on the last ship. We mustn't untie the ships until every sail's been reefed, and should a ship break away from the fleet, no one is to go after it. That's how you must sail. No matter what happens, no matter what you think you see, you must not disobey my orders, and then everything will be all right. We mustn't go ashore, or break our journey at all, until we reach Russia. Now, let's hoist sail, there's no shortage of good winds.'

Everything was done as Mondul had ordered. Earl Thorgny and Ingigerd bade them farewell, and Counsellor Bjorn stayed behind with the Earl to help govern the country.

Then a favourable wind sprang up, and Hrolf sailed off with his fleet. They made little headway at first but soon they saw signs in the sky that the weather was changing. The sea around them became choppy, and they heard loud rumblings in the air. Mondul sat at the helm on the last ship. He took a large stick, tied a blue string round it, and towed it in the ship's wake.

One night a war fleet appeared to be making for Hrolf's ship, as if about to launch an attack. Mondul called out and told them to pay no attention to it, but they said he was just too scared to defend Hrolf and his crew. They detached one of the ships from the fleet and tried to get ahead of the rest, but that proved impossible for they were hit by a headwind which drove the ship back far behind all the others. The last anyone saw of the ship was when a huge walrus came up and over-turned it, drowning every man aboard. They had many other strange experiences, and people didn't take them all in the same way. Alto-gether they lost twenty ships before they reached Russia.

They sailed up the River Dvina, plundering both banks, burning settlements and looting everything they could lay hands on. Many submitted to them, and in that way they added considerably to their forces. It wasn't long before they heard where King Eirik was to be found with a large army. They brought their ships in to a certain anchorage, where Mondul got himself a boat and rowed round the fleet. After that he went ashore and told the men to make camp close to a nearby cliff. 'Each tent must be pitched against the next,' he said, and that's how it was done.

Then he untied his bundle, and out of it he took black tents, made of silk. These he pitched firmly over the other tents, covering them so completely that there wasn't the smallest gap visible. They had arrived in Russia just about Winter Eves.[1]

'Now,' said the dwarf Mondul, 'we must unload the ships and carry into the tents enough provisions to last us for three days. Then you must go inside the tents and not even look out of them until I give you the word.'

Everything was done as he ordered. Mondul was the last to go inside, but only after he'd walked around the tents. A little later they heard the wind blowing harder and beating fiercely against the tents. They

---

1. *vetrnaetr*. According to the Icelandic calendar, summer ends on a Thursday, and winter begins the following Saturday. The intervening days were called 'Winter Eves', but the term is sometimes used loosely in the sense of 'the beginning of winter'.

thought this very weird. One of them was so curious that he lifted the edge of the tent and took a peep outside. By the time that he'd drawn his head back in, he'd been struck dumb and gone raving mad, and not long after that he died.

The weather stayed the same for three days.

'We shan't all of us succeed in making it back to Denmark, if Grim Aegir has his way,' said Mondul. 'He was the walrus that sank our ships; and he'd have treated them all the same, if I hadn't been in the last ship, but he couldn't get beyond the stick I had in tow. Now he's worked up this blizzard against you, and you'd all have been killed, if the tents hadn't been there to protect you. On top of that, twelve men have come into the wood nearby, sent by Grim to King Eirik. They've travelled from Ermland, and they're busy working a spell against you, Hrolf and Stefnir, to make you kill each other. So let seven of us go and visit them and see what happens.'

They did what he advised and entered the wood where they saw a house. Coming from it they could hear the horrible noise made by the sorcerers. Hrolf and his men went into the house, and there they saw a high platform resting on four columns. Mondul went under the plat-form, and carved counter-spells so powerful they even worked on the sorcerers. After that they went back into the wood and waited for a while, but the sorcerers were so confused that they smashed up the platform and ran screaming out of the house, all in different directions. Some ran into a swamp or the sea, others jumped off a cliff, or over a precipice; and that's how they all died. Hrolf and his men went back to the fleet and saw all the ships in a healthy condition. The blizzard, they realised, had raged no further than the ships and the tents.

'Here's how matters stand, Hrolf,' said Mondul. 'I'm taking no part in the battle, as I've neither the strength for it, nor the courage. Still, you'd not have had much of an army left, if you'd been the only one in charge. You and Stefnir were supposed to die just like the sorcerers.'

They thanked him for his magic, and got ready to go ashore.

CHAPTER 29

Death of Earl Thorgny

SOON AFTER HROLF and his men set out for Russia from Jutland, the berserk Tryggvi, whom we've already mentioned, turned up with an army too big to be beaten. After flying from Hrolf and Stefnir, he'd spent most of the time in Scotland and England, but now he'd heard how they had left the country and he knew there wouldn't be many left to defend it.

As soon as he got news of the invasion, Earl Thorgny gathered forces, but Tryggvi had attacked without warning and the best men were all away, so the Earl could raise only a small force. They came face to face a short distance from town, and at once a savage battle broke out, both sides fighting bravely. Earl Thorgny had his banner carried forward boldly, going close behind it himself, fighting fiercely and killing a good many men. Counsellor Bjorn followed him staunchly, killing men by the score, for both these men were courageous and war-seasoned warriors. But Tryggvi was fighting well, too, raging through the Earl's ranks, so that nothing could withstand him, and soon the Earl and his men began to lose ground. The battle lasted all day, but in the end, with great honour, Earl Thorgny fell, and it was Tryggvi who gave him his deathblow. Then Bjorn the Counsellor fled with the survivors back to the town, and there they stayed while Tryggvi laid siege to it.

Late in the evening they saw three ships making for land, big ones with black gunwales. They dropped anchor and set up the awnings. The townsmen were deeply troubled about the way things were going. In the morning, the crews marched up to the town in battle order. There were twelve men in the lead, two of them wearing masks over their faces. Tryggvi formed up, but when they met, they didn't have much to say in the way of greetings, for the masked men attacked at once, making a brave fight of it. When the townsmen saw this, they marched outside the walls and went for the enemy from behind. Tryggvi was caught between the two, and as the attackers pressed hard against him, his troops were cut down in vast numbers. When the end came, he and most of his men were dead, and a great deal of plunder was taken. At once the masked men went back to their ships without a word to anyone. The people of the town were utterly perplexed by all this, and wondered who these men could be, but no one could tell them. Afterwards, now that all was quiet, a burial mound was raised for Earl Thorgny. Thora grieved bitterly over her father's death, and many other people felt the same, for he'd been a good chieftain and ruler, and had governed the counrty long and well, and enjoyed a peaceful reign, which is why everyone felt it to be a great loss when he was killed.

CHAPTER 30

First day of battle

NOW WE'D BETTER get on with the story where we left off earlier, with Hrolf directing all his forces against King Eirik. They met not far from the town of Ladoga. The King's army was a massive one, and very formidable, including as it did many great men. One was an Earl called Imi, a big strong man, and a good fighter. He was a Russian by birth, and with him was his half-brother, Rondolf, so huge and powerful that he ought rightly to be called a troll. His mother's family belonged to Aluborg in Giantland, and that's where he'd been reared. The club he used for a weapon was six ells long, with a great bulge at one end. Scarcely any weapon could bite the coat he was wearing. When he grew angry, Rondolf would burst into a frenzy and howl like a troll. Brynjolf was also with the King, but Thord and Grim were gathering forces in the upper part of the country and hadn't arrived yet.

Both sides made camp and slept through the night on a level plain, close by the sea. Early in the morning they prepared for battle. The King arranged his army in two columns, leading one of them himself with Brynjolf carrying his banner, and Rondolf and all the greatest warriors going ahead of it. In the second column were Earl Imi and other great men not mentioned by name. Imi's banner was carried by a man called Arnodd, a great champion. Hrolf also arranged his troops into two columns. He led one of them against King Eirik, and under his banner he had Swedes and Frisians. Stefnir led the other column, made up of Jutes. Ali was the name of his standard-bearer, the greatest of fighters. Hrolf was wearing Hreggvid's armour and riding Dulcifal. In each army there was a large troop of cavalry. Stefnir was wearing one of Hrolf's cloaks; but because Mondul was unaccustomed to arms, he took no part in the battle.

That was how both armies were disposed as they shouted the warcry, and the columns closed in on each other. At once a fierce battle was joined with heavy loss of life on both sides. After a cavalry attack came sharp hand-to-hand combat, hewing and thrusting. Rondolf advanced boldly, striking right and left with the club, and killing both men and horses. There wasn't a knight strong enough to take a blow from him, and he cleared everything in his path. Brynjolf carried the banner forward boldly and there was a lot of unhappy murmuring in Hrolf's ranks. Hrolf himself was forging ahead on Dulcifal, and there was no man staunch enough to stay in the saddle under Hrolf's stroke. He kept slashing with Hreggvid's sword at men and horses alike, killing many, for the sword bit as if it were slicing through water, and showed no sign of faltering in its stroke. The battle was so fierce that men were being slaughtered in heaps.

Now the story goes that Stefnir rode hard forward into Earl Imi's ranks, causing great harm to many a knight, till at last Earl Imi came against him. Each thrusting at the other's shield, they charged furiously. When they met, Imi's spearshaft snapped in the middle, and Stefnir struck him, knocking him backwards right out of the saddle and well away from the horse. Quickly Imi was on his feet and drew his sword. Stefnir leapt from his horse and hewed at him. He hit back, but Stefnir's sword caught the hilt and sliced off Imi's hand. Then Stefnir ran him through; and that's how Imi died. Stefnir carried on fighting briskly.

Elsewhere Ali and Arnodd had come face to face and were attacking each other boldly. They went on hewing away at each other until all their protective armour was shattered to bits. Each of them had dropped his banner, and the fight ended like this: Arnodd plunged his sword into Ali's guts right through the back, but Ali walked straight into the thrust striking with both hands at Arnodd's head so that the blow split his skull to the teeth, and both men fell dead.

At this point Hrolf, seeing what havoc Rondolf was causing among his troops, decided to bear it no longer. He leapt off Dulcifal and rushed up to Rondolf. As they met, Rondolf struck at Hrolf with the iron-studded club, but Hrolf dodged the heavy blow, which might, he thought, be too much even for him. The stroke landed on two men who'd been standing behind Hrolf and smashed every bone in their bodies. Taking a swipe with his sword at Rondolf's arm, Hrolf cut off his hand at the wrist and all the toes on one foot. Rondolf raised the club high in the air with one hand and struck at Hrolf with all his strength. The club buried itself up to half its length in the ground, but Hrolf wasn't touched. Then Hrolf cut off Rondolf's other hand, and as it dropped to the ground Rondolf turned away, waving both stumps and bellowing like a bull. After that Hrolf sliced off both his buttocks, so that they hung by the skin from the hollows of the knees, and trailing this load behind him, he charged bellowing into King Eirik's ranks.

96

Everyone tried to get out from in front of him, but he still managed to kill a good many men this way.

Hrolf and Stefnir and their men made good use of this advantage, striking and thrusting at all before them. King Eirik's troops were going down in heaps. Rondolf didn't care what stood in his way. He charged into Brynjolf, knocking him flat along with his banner, but Brynjolf managed to scramble to his feet again and run off. Once King Eirik's men realised that the banner was down, they all made off, every single one of them. When King Eirik saw this he ran back to town like the rest, but Hrolf and Stefnir followed up the rout, killing everyone they could. The casualties were so heavy that they couldn't be counted. Rondolf ran into the river and drowned himself, but King Eirik and the survivors with him barricaded themselves in the town; and that's how the battle ended. The time was just about dusk.

Hrolf went back to his camp and had the wounded seen to. A good many of his men had also been killed. Late in the evening Hrolf's men saw three warships approaching land; they sailed into the anchorage and lay there. Then three hundred men came ashore from the ships, all of them brave-looking, and well-equipped, and their leader was the biggest of all. They went to Hrolf's camp, and meeting them, Hrolf realised that they were his father Sturlaug and his brother Eirik, so there was a grand reunion between them. Hrolf asked his father for news of his travels. By this time Sturlaug was getting very old and had long given up warlike expeditions. He said he'd heard all about Hrolf's adventures, and it was to help Hrolf that he'd set out from Norway for Russia. They spent the rest of the evening drinking and enjoying themselves. Sturlaug had his armour and Vefreyja's shortsword, and with him were many great warriors and champions from Ringerike, one called Torfi the Strong, the second Bard, the third Gardi, the fourth Atli, the fifth Birgir, the sixth Solvir, the seventh Lodin, and the eighth Knut Kveisa. All these were the bravest of fighting men, but Torfi and Knut were supposed by far to surpass even the others. So they went to sleep, but kept a close watch throughout the night.

CHAPTER 31
Second day of battle

DURING THE NIGHT, massive reinforcements came to join King Eirik from the neighbouring districts, and that same evening Grim Aegir and Thord Laeso-Pate had turned up with countless fighting men including many champions and berserks, twelve of these being named. One was called Orn the Ermlander, the second Ulf, and along with them Har, Gellir, Sorli Long-Nose, Tjorfi, Tjosnir, Lodmund, Haki, Lifolf, Styr the Strong and Brusi Bone-Shirt, all hard to handle and more like trolls than men; four were the most evil of the lot, namely Tjosnir and Gellir, and the brothers Styr and Brusi. King Eirik was delighted they'd come and told them about the great losses he'd suffered, and how there was none to compare with Hrolf for courage and the quality of his weapons.

'It was a great blow to us when Hrolf got Hreggvid's sword,' said Eirik.

'Things may still be all right,' said Grim. 'Tomorrow we'll make up for the losses you suffered today.'

The night passed, and at dawn both sides prepared for battle. King Eirik marched out of the town with all his troops and formed up in battle-order. Brynjolf was still carrying his banner, and under it were eight berserks: Orn the Ermlander, Ulf, Har, Sorli, Lifolf, Lodmund, Herkir, and Tjorfi. Grim Aegir went ahead of the banner. On the other flank was Thord Laeso-Plate, with a banner carried before him. Along with Thord were Tjosnir, Gellir, Styr, Brusi and many others.

Hrolf and Stefnir formed up to meet King Eirik. With them were Knut Kveisa and Torfi the Strong. Against Thord came a formation led by Sturlaug and his son Eirik, and these six champions: Hadd, Gardi, Atli, Birgir, Solvi and Lodin. It's not mentioned who the standard-bearers were, apart from Brynjolf. The odds greatly favoured King Eirik, who had three men to every one of his opponents. Then the trumpets sounded, and the columns drove at one another, shouting encouragement and clashing their weapons. First came a fierce shower of missiles, then hand-to-hand fighting began, each side raging against the other. Everything was happening all at once, but we can only tell one story at a time. Mondul the dwarf wasn't on the battlefield, but standing on a hill, shooting away with a handbow and doing a lot of damage. Both sides moved forward bravely, and no man's courage was in any doubt. Together Knut Kveisa and Torfi the Strong, both powerful men and skilled in witchcraft, attacked Grim Aegir for most of the day. They clashed so fiercely that every man near them had to run for his life. The King's berserks caused great havoc too, striding so hard through Hrolf's ranks that everyone gave way before them. Many a good warrior lost his authority in that struggle; no helmet was so sturdy or shield so strong that it could withstand their strokes. The state of Hrolf's army came close to rout.

Hrolf had advanced into King Eirik's ranks with Stefnir at his side, and they'd done a great deal of damage. Then they saw how strongly the berserks were surging forward, so back they turned to confront them. When they met, neither side could have asked for strokes any mightier than those given. Hrolf struck at Orn, but as he tried to ward off the blow with his shield, the sword sliced through, and the point ripped open the whole of his belly so that his guts poured out. Next Hrolf ran Herkir through and cut both legs off Lifolf. Stefnir stabbed at Ulf with a spear; and, as Ulf thrust his shield against it, the spear pierced right through into his thigh, wounding him badly. Ulf cut the spear-head off the shaft. Har pounced on Hrolf and struck him on the helm with a nail-studded club, knocking him almost unconscious: yet still Hrolf managed to turn on Ulf and thrust at him with the sword. The mailcoat failed, and the sword went right through him. Lodmund lunged at Stefnir and hit him in the calf, piercing it through. Just at that moment, Hrolf came up and, making a two-handed stroke at Lodmund's head, sliced him through, so that the sword stuck in the ground. Then Sorli and Tjorfi set on Hrolf, and Har let fly at his back with the club. That would have been his death had the cloak and armour not protected him; even so, he was still beaten down on both knees. He sprang to his feet quickly and struck at Har, slicing through his leg at the knee. Hrolf took a swing with the sword at Tjorfi's side and cut him clean through at the waist. After that Sorli tried to make off. Har had got up onto one leg and begun hitting out with the club at anything near him. He killed eleven men before Stefnir dealt him his deathblow, and there, with all honour, his life came to an end. Now the battle was growing fierce, and many were killed by King Eirik and Brynjolf; then Mondul's arrow pierced King Eirik through the arm.

Now that their side was losing the battle, Hrolf and Stefnir made a fresh onslaught, and reached the spot where Grim Aegir was fighting Torfi and Knut. All about them the earth had been churned up. The upshot of the fight was that Torfi lay wounded and helpless, and Knut lay dead. By that time Grim was exhausted, having been the death of a good many men. Together Hrolf and Stefnir struck at him, but he slipped away into the earth, just as if he were diving into water.

While all this was taking place, Sturlaug and his men marched against the other flank. Each side waded through the other's ranks with great sword strokes and massive spear thrusts, causing fearful carnage. Sturlaug kept lunging and hewing to right and left with Vefreyja's short-sword. No one who got a scratch from him needed to worry himself about dressing his wounds. Eirik his son followed him close, felling man after man. Thord Laeso-Pate went like a champion against Sturlaug, baring his naked skull, but though they struck at it with swords and axes, they made no mark, and he went forward unshaken. The Norwegians, forty of Sturlaug's men, turned on him together, but he held them off like a true hero.

Elsewhere Styr the Strong and Brusi Bone-Shirt were in the field, and against them came Hadd and Gard, Birgir and Solvir. These four men set on the other two and needed all the hands they'd got. Though their strokes and thrusts aren't recorded in every detail, their onslaught was hard and bitter. The outcome was that after killing Hadd and Gard, cutting off both Solvi's hands, and giving Birgir a bad wound, Styr and Brusi fell exhausted. Solvi rushed up to one of the enemy and, smashing his head into the man's chest, burst his ribs and killed him. Another man he first knocked flat, then bit out his throat, but afterwards they ran Solvi through with a spear; and so he died, like a true hero.

Lodin and Atli set on Gellir, but it was a fierce struggle, for he was a real monster, and stood up against them despite a good many wounds. He lunged at Atli with the point of his halberd, striking him on the helmet and so right into the brain. Lodin wanted revenge and thrusting his sword through Gellir's mailcoat, gave him a deep wound in the thigh. Next Gellir struck at Lodin. The blow snapped his collarbone, slicing his heart in two, and there he died. Then Eirik Sturlaugsson came up and gave Gellir his deathblow.

Now Tjosnir and Sturlaug met. Though both landed blows, neither was wounded. Sturlaug shattered Tjosnir's shield, but had to fall back before his great strides. Mondul saw this. He put a barbed arrow to his bowstring and shot it so deep into Tjosnir's eye that it went in right to the end of the shaft. Tjosnir grabbed at the arrow to pull it out, and out came the eye with it. Sturlaug made the most of his chance and split Tjosnir right down the middle, the two halves toppling to either side.

Sturlaug saw the great damage Thord was doing him, what with his men nearly routed and a number of them dead. He sought out Thord, who turned to meet him, and a long and bitter combat followed between them before Sturlaug could land a blow. It caught Thord on

101

the pate and the sword proved as good as ever, for it split his head wide open and went straight through the trunk, so that he fell to the ground in two halves. But Sturlaug had gone too far this time, for his short-sword shot down deep into the earth and was never seen again. As to these events, books don't agree at all. According to *Sturlaug's Saga* and other tales as well, Sturlaug died in his bed at home in Ringerike and was buried there in a mound, but here it's stated that after Thord's death Grim Aegir came up out of the ground behind Sturlaug and sliced him through with a sword. We can't say which comes nearer the truth.

Sturlaug's son Eirik saw all this, for he was standing close by. In a fury he swung with his sword at Grim's shoulder, but the sword cracked as if it had struck a stone, and didn't bite at all. Grim turned against Eirik and spewed such hot venom into his face that he dropped down dead. The sight of this terrified every man there, yet still the battle raged, and the slaughter continued.

When Hrolf learned this, he flew into a rage and gave Hreggvid's sword no rest, but struck so hard and fast that everyone scattered from his path. Sometimes he would kill two or three at a single stroke, then surge forward like a man wading through a torrent. The battle lasted all day, until it was too dark to fight. Then King Eirik had the shield of peace hoisted, and the fighting came to an end. The King went back to town with his troops, and Hrolf to his camp to dress the wounds of those whose lives might be saved. By now so many of Hrolf and Stefnir's great host had been slaughtered that there were scarcely more than two thousand left alive, most of them badly wounded, and the men had begun to complain bitterly. But after their hard labour they took their rest, and soon they were all asleep.

CHAPTER 32

Visit to Hreggvid

A S SOON AS his men were asleep, Hrolf got up very quietly, walked over to Dulcifal, mounted him, and rode all the way to Hreggvid's mound. It was bright moonlight. Hrolf dismounted and climbed up the mound. He saw that Hreggvid was sitting outside, gazing at the moon. This is what he was singing:

Hreggvid is glad:
bold Hrolf is here,
come to Russia
to bring good cheer,
and dare what no
man else may do,
avenge my death
on Eirik's crew.

Hreggvid is glad.
The days are sped
for Grim, and Thord
will soon be dead.
All of my foes
go to the wall;
Hrolf and Fate
will see them fall.

Hreggvid is glad
that Hrolf will wed
his pretty maid,
young Ingigerd.
Soon Sturlaug's son
shall rule this land.
My song is sung,
my words will stand.

Then Hrolf came forward and gave him a respectful greeting, which the King returned in a friendly way, asking how he was getting on.

'You'll know all about that already, so I don't have to tell you,' said Hrolf. 'What with all the losses we've suffered, the battle's been going badly for us so far. Now it's up to you to give us some good advice and rescue us.'

'I'm not worried,' said Hreggvid. 'No matter how unlikely it may seem at the moment, you'll be able to avenge me and win the victory. Here are two vats which you're to take with you: give drinks from one of them to all your men as soon as they wake in the morning, and you and Stefnir drink from the other. After that you'll never have any disagreements. And there's something else I can tell you. As soon as Stefnir saw how beautiful my daughter Ingigerd was, he made up his mind to marry her, and not let you or his father Thorgny have her. But I want her to be your wife, and once you've both drunk from the vat, Stefnir isn't going to argue the point with you. Here's a knife, too, and a belt I want you to have; there's nothing like them anywhere in Scandinavia. Give them to nobody but the one you really owe a debt to. We're going to part now, and we'll never meet again. I want you to cover up the mound the way I've shown you. Give my love to my daughter Ingigerd. May you have all the good luck that used to be mine! Goodbye now, I hope everything will go just as you wish.'

Then Hreggvid walked backwards into the mound. Hrolf covered it up as he'd been told, mounted Dulcifal, and rode back to the camp.

When he'd almost reached the camp, Stefnir came to meet him fully armed and in a great rage. 'You've played me a dirty trick,' he said, 'going to Hreggvid's mound and grabbing all the credit for yourself. I suppose you think this will help you to get Princess Ingigerd, but that's far from settled yet.'

'It's not glory I've been after,' said Hrolf, 'even though I did travel further than you last night. I've never set my mind on the Princess; and no matter what people think, the fact remains that the one who gets her will be the one who's destined to.'

Then Hrolf told Stefnir about his visit to the mound and showed him the vats. They sat down to drink from one of them, and both felt very much stronger for it. Stefnir grew friendly towards Hrolf and told him he deserved to have Ingigerd. 'You're a much more proper man to marry her than that old fellow, my father,' he said.

They went back to camp and slept for the rest of the night.

Early in the morning Hrolf roused his troops and made everyone drink from the vat. Once they'd all had a taste, not one among them was troubled by his wounds any more, not even those who'd been unfit for fighting before they'd settled down to drink, and the ones who had wanted to run away were now the keenest for battle.

Mondul looked into the vat and called it a very friendly gesture. 'But I don't want to drink any of this ale,' he said. 'You can all become fearsome fighters now. A great feast will be waiting for us at the end of the day, and you'll have some tales to tell.'

They armed themselves, and everyone got ready for battle.

'The day's come, Hrolf,' said Mondul, 'when you're really going to need your cloak, and here's a brown silk scarf to put under the hood. Never raise it from your face, no matter how hot it makes you.'

Hrolf took the scarf, and put it on as the dwarf had told him to. Then they went to the battlefield, formed up, and showed themselves ready for the fight. They had chosen a new battlefield, as the old one was littered with corpses and couldn't be used any more. Mondul walked widdershins twice round the dead, whistling and blowing in all directions, mumbling ancient chants, and declaring that these dead warriors must do no harm.

CHAPTER 33

Third day of battle

AFTER THE PREVIOUS DAY'S BATTLE was over, King Eirik had gone into town that night to have his men's wounds seen to. He'd suffered heavy casualties, including the loss of all his champions, except for Sorli Long-Nose, the only one left alive of all those who'd come to the battle with Grim and Thord, but still a great host of fighting men flocked to him from the settlements, by night and day. He and Grim Aegir thought that with the odds so much in their favour, they could do what they liked with Hrolf and his men. Grim and Brynjolf made all sorts of magical preparations during the night. The wound King Eirik had received in the arm from Mondul's arrow had swollen badly, and he couldn't fight with that hand.

Early in the morning King Eirik rode out of the town with all his troops. After he had arranged his formations, a shield wall was formed around him. Brynjolf had the task of defending it, and a man called Snak carried the banner. On the other flank were Grim Aegir and Sorli Long-Nose. The odds were so one-sided they'd six men to each one of Hrolf's.

When Hrolf realised this, he told his men not to form up. 'Instead we'll attack them in small detachments, thirty or forty to a group, so that they can't surround us with this host of men they've got. I'll set about Grim Aegir, and Stefnir and Torfi will attack King Eirik. But I'm going to rely on you, Mondul, to deal with Grim's magic, and make sure he doesn't kill our men with witchcraft.'

Mondul stepped forward, wearing a black coat completely covering his body. Under one arm he carried a huge bag made of yellow cloth, with a deerskin lining. In the other hand he had a bow and quiver. Everyone thought his outfit looked very strange.

Grim went across to where the corpses were lying and began rolling them over, for he wanted to raise them from the dead, but found he couldn't. Then the expression on his face grew so horrible that scarcely a soul dared look at him, for his eyes blazed like fire, and black smoke poured from his mouth and nostrils with a horrible stench.

At once the two armies shouted the warcry and set upon one another. Grim bellowed so loudly that his screams could be heard even above the warcry. He ran in front of his column, and as he made for Hrolf's men, he started shaking the bag he had, so that a cloud of dust flew from it. When Mondul saw this, he stepped forward and, shaking his own bag, made a fierce gale blow from it at the dust cloud, sweeping it back towards Grim's men and right into their eyes, blinding them, so that they fell and were trampled to death by their own troops. This put Grim into a rage. Putting an arrow to his bowstring, he shot it at Mondul, but Mondul aimed one back, and meeting point to point, the two arrows dropped to the ground. Altogether, this happened three times.

While all this was going on, the main battle continued to rage with shouting and clamour, each man urging on his companions, for Hrolf's men were so eager they spared nothing and acted as if certain of victory. Stefnir fought well against King Eirik, along with Torfi and Birgir. They surged ahead and it would take far too long to describe every blow they struck, for the men they killed were countless. Brynjolf was fighting bravely too, along with Sval, the standard-bearer, and together they brought down forty fighters in the first onslaught. Hrolf came up against Grim Aegir and hewed at him, but Grim fell back, then took off into the air in the form of a winged dragon, spewing venom over Hrolf. Mondul was near at hand and put his bag underneath to catch the venom. Then he ran with the bag at Sorli Long-Nose and threw it right into his face, so that Sorli dropped down dead. Next

Grim turned back into human shape once more, but only after he'd killed nine men with the poison. Grim ran up to seize the dwarf, but Mondul didn't care to wait for him and dived down into the earth right where he was. Grim plunged after him, and the ground closed over their heads.

Hrolf advanced hard, hewing left and right, and sweeping men from his path, so that they fell in heaps. The moment Hrolf's sword came within reach of any man, a single blow was enough to transform life into death. Hrolf's arms were drenched in blood up to the shoulders, and most men shunned him in terror. There was carnage on both flanks of the battle.

Then some of the fighters saw fifteen ships pulling at full speed towards the coast. They sailed into harbour and numbers of men poured ashore, all very warlike. Two of them were taller than the rest, and wore masks over their faces. At once these troops joined Hrolf and began to fight. They took King Eirik very much by surprise, and his army began to scatter. The masked men were the most aggressive of all, striking hard and fast, and now the battle was fiercer than ever. Many a good shield was shattered there, many strong helmets were crushed, mailcoats torn to shreds, and great men laid low. No one had time to heed another's warning. The air was thick with missiles, as men flung spears and javelins, darts and daggers.

Hrolf strode towards the shield wall, but met stout resistance. Grim Aegir rejoined the battle with an ugly look on his face, killing all who came his way. Birgir, Torfi, and the two masked men went after him keenly, all four of them, but couldn't inflict a single wound. He dealt them many a hard blow, wounding them and wearing them down.

At that same moment, Stefnir met Sval and hewed at him with a sword. The blow took a slice out of his shield, and severed the standard pole. Sval struck back at him, splitting the shield, but Stefnir wasn't harmed. Again he struck out at Sval, catching the side of the helmet, so that the sword glanced off the brim and into the shoulder, cracking the bone, and so into the chest. Sval died on the spot, and now King Eirik's banner lay in the grass.

When Brynjolf saw this, he sought out Stefnir, with a fierce look about him, his teeth set like a wild boar's. Each hewed away at the other, but nothing could bite through Vefreyja's cloak, nor could Stefnir's sword bite Brynjolf. After they had battled with one another for some time, Stefnir began to tire, and then his sword snapped at the hilt. He threw himself at Brynjolf, and the pair grappled furiously. Brynjolf bit into Stefnir's shoulder, mumbling all the flesh about the bone that his teeth could take, but because the cloak covered it, he couldn't bite through. Stefnir took this like a man, thrust his hand into Brynjolf's mouth, and tore it wide open to the ear, which made him less than kissable. For a long time they struggled, with now one, now the other giving way. Then Brynjolf tripped over Sval's body and fell flat on his back, but he clasped his hands around Stefnir, so that Stefnir couldn't budge an inch, and had to keep his face turned aside to stop Brynjolf from biting it.

Now we come back to Hrolf, fiercely assaulting the shield wall. Many were the strokes and lunges and thrusts he had to take, as all King Eirik's bravest men were gathered there. Hrolf would have suffered many wounds and injuries, had the cloak's armour not shielded him. It was then that Hrolf alone killed seventy horsemen, and smashed the shield wall. King Eirik defended himself well and bravely, and called out loud for Grim Aegir to make every effort to help him. When Grim heard this, he hurried over. He'd already killed Torfi and Birgir and wounded both of the masked men, one of them fatally. At various times he'd changed himself into a winged dragon, a serpent, a wild boar, a bull – any dangerous beast that's harmful to men.

When Hrolf saw him, he said, 'I suppose you want to dive into the earth again, as you did when we met yesterday? If you have the stomach for it, Aegir, come and fight me to the death.'

'You'll soon know I'm here,' said Grim; and with that he and Hrolf clashed. You might have seen some hard blows there, many a giant stroke, yet none enough to bite the other man. So fierce was the fight, sparks flew everywhere from their swords, and everyone near them ran for cover.

The tall masked man went bitterly against King Eirik. Eirik carried his shield in his injured hand, striking with the other hard and fast, great champion that he was, but in the end the masked man shattered the King's shield, then sliced off both legs, and killed him; and so King Eirik fell, like a true hero. After that, his army took to its heels, every man for himself, and as the vikings raced eagerly after them, the slaughter began all over again.

Hrolf and Grim Aegir withdrew from the battle but went on fighting like heroes till Hrolf managed to cut Grim's blade through the middle with Hreggvid's sword. Grim threw all his weight against Hrolf, so Hrolf had to drop the sword and grapple with him. In his frenzy, Grim waded up to his knees in earth, but Hrolf kept backing away from him to avoid being flattened. Grim spewed venom at Hrolf one moment, and fire the next, and had Hrolf not been wearing his cloak and the scarf Mondul had given him, he could never have survived. Grim's breath was so hot, Hrolf thought his whole body was aflame, despite Vefreyja's cloak and the armour he wore. Grim squeezed the flesh off his bones wherever he could grasp him, and Hrolf couldn't remember when he'd last had such a rough time. He knew that if the two of them went on struggling much longer, he'd collapse with exhaustion. They braced their feet so hard against the earth that grass and turf churned up wherever they went. Then Hrolf saw Mondul race up. The dwarf picked up a sword lying there on the field, and hewed with both hands at Grim's leg, but the stroke bit no deeper than if it had struck a rock. Mondul ran back to the battlefield and found Hreggvid's sword lying there. He smeared the edge with his spittle, and though it was too heavy for him to carry, dragged it over to the place where Grim and Hrolf

110

were battling, drew the blade across Grim's calves, and cut the tendons. Grim fell to the ground.

'Hold onto him, Hrolf!' said the dwarf. 'Don't let him break loose!'

Grim put up a great struggle and tried to slip away into the earth, but Hrolf held him back with all the strength he had. Then Grim Aegir spoke.

'It's amazing good luck you have, Hrolf,' he said; 'and you'll make a great name for yourself by killing me, and for all your other deeds here in Russia. I want a burial mound raised over me, close by the sea, and should any voyager land there, death will be his destiny. I've laid a good many traps to kill you, but I've always had a sense this would happen. I sent William to trick you, but you weren't fated to die. Even so, you wouldn't have beaten me if that damned dwarf hadn't been here to help you.'

Mondul jumped to his feet and drove a thick piece of wood into Grim's mouth so that it stuck firm. 'If we'd let Grim speak another word', said Mondul, 'he'd have laid such a curse on you and the rest, you'd all have crumbled down into nothing but dust. You'd better kill him at once. Thrust your sword right into his breast, but don't cut his limbs off. Everything that's cut off him turns into poisonous snakes. And no one must look him in the face when he's dying – that would mean death for sure.'

Hrolf took Hreggvid's sword, then drove it into Grim's chest and out through his back, while the dwarf took a shield and placed it over his face. And, strange as it must seem, the story goes that Grim melted away like snow in a flame and crumbled into nothing but dust. That's how Grim Aegir died, in violent death agonies, lashing about with his fists like a madman: but Hrolf lay on top of him till he was quite dead. After the struggle he'd had with Grim Aegir, Hrolf was barely conscious for some time.

The tall masked man turned back to the battlefield after he'd chased the fleeing enemy, and came to the spot where earlier we left Stefnir

111

and Brynjolf lying. He wanted to help Stefnir and tried to loosen Brynjolf's grip on him, but couldn't until he'd broken every one of his fingers. Then they battered Brynjolf with cudgels till he was dead. Stefnir was so stiff from Brynjolf's grip, he could barely walk on his own two legs.

That was the end of the great battle; and there was such slaughter there that no one had ever heard of anything like it. Corpses were strewn so thick over the battlefield one couldn't move for them. King Eirik had lost more men than Hrolf and Stefnir, yet even they had lost all but a mere eight hundred, and most survivors were wounded. There was no shortage of weapons now, or of other plunder that had belonged to the dead. Hrolf and Stefnir went back to their camp, and Mondul the dwarf set to and dressed the wounded, everyone praising his skill and energy. Mondul said that when he plunged down into the earth, it would have been certain death if Grim had caught him.

'It saved me,' he said. 'I had more friends down there than he had.'

The masked man went with his men down to his ships in the evening, and there they made camp. After that everyone went to sleep and most of them thought it was about time. Those of Eirik's troops who had escaped fled into the town and waited there.

CHAPTER 34

The masked man

DURING THE NIGHT, when everyone was asleep, Hrolf and Stefnir went down to the other camp, where all the men lay sleeping in their armour. Taking the knife and the belt that Hreggvid had given him, Hrolf tied them to the masked man's spearshaft, and said, 'These gifts I offer to the leader of this force, and thank him for his generous help and support. Any favour in my power that he'd care to ask of me, I feel bound to grant him.'

There was no answer, so back they went to their camp and slept through the night.

Early in the morning Hrolf went up to the town with his men, and the masked man joined him there with his own forces. Hrolf summoned the townsmen to a meeting and offered them a truce if they would give up the town, so they did. Hrolf went into the town with all his men and held an assembly there, where Hrolf announced that they had come on behalf of Princess Ingigerd to win back her Kingdom from her enemies. He added that she was staying in Denmark, in good health and good hands. Everyone was pleased to hear this and said they'd be glad to live under her rule.

Hrolf and his men went over to the palace and began drinking and enjoying themselves. Then the stranger took off his mask, and Hrolf and Stefnir recognised him as that Hrafn who'd once been in Jutland, and Hrolf had given clothes to. He told them all the news from Denmark – that Earl Thorgny was dead, and that he'd been there himself when it happened. Hrolf and Stefnir were saddened by this but thanked him handsomely for all his help.

Hrafn said he'd been afraid the day before that he might have come too late. 'I owe you a lot for saving my life and giving me those clothes that time,' he said. 'And it was Grim Aegir who killed my brother Krak, a great loss but one I shall have to bear.'

They said nothing more about that, and spent the night there enjoying themselves.

In the morning Hrolf and his men had the battlefields cleared, and divided the spoils between them. Then three great burial mounds were raised. In one of them Hrolf laid Sturlaug, his father, and Krak, Hrafn's brother, and all the bravest heroes on their side who'd fallen there.

Into this mound they carried gold and silver and fine weapons and laid everything out very properly. In the second mound they laid King

113

Eirik, Brynjolf, Thord, and all their henchmen. And in the third one, close by the sea, they laid Grim Aegir, at a place where they thought it least likely that any ship might come to land. The common folk were all buried just where they'd been killed.

Hrolf appointed men to govern the whole kingdom until the Princess came back. The dwarf took leave of Hrolf, who thanked him for his help and gave him everything he asked for. King Eirik's sister Gyda vanished from Russia, and some people have guessed that it must have been Mondul who carried her off.

After that Hrolf and his men got ready to sail back home from Russia, and didn't stop until they got to Aarhus in Denmark, the town Earl Thorgny had fortified more strongly than any other. Bjorn came out to welcome them warmly, as did all the people there. The young ladies were particularly pleased to see them back, and Ingigerd thanked them for the way they'd fought. Bjorn had kept the women in an underground chamber after the Earl's death.

Ingigerd announced bluntly that she'd take no one as her husband but Hrolf Sturlaugsson, since he'd done more than anyone to avenge her father – 'and now he's lost his father, his brother, kinsmen and friends, and risked his life in the most terrible danger'.

No one raised any objection, and Bjorn laid out a splendid feast to celebrate Earl Thorgny's funeral.

CHAPTER 35

Hrafn's story

ONE DAY DURING the feast, Hrafn got to his feet and asked for a hearing.

'I'd like to thank you, Hrolf and Stefnir,' he said, 'for all the honour and hospitality you've shown me on this occasion, and during my previous stay here. Now I want to tell you my name and family. There was a king called Edgar who ruled over a certain kingdom in England and had his main seat in a town called Winchester. He had two sons and one daughter. His elder son was called Harald, his younger Sigurd, and his daughter Alfhild. I am Harald, but my brother Sigurd was killed in Russia, as you know. My mother's family belongs here in Denmark. When I was fifteen and my brother thirteen, my father was betrayed by a kinsman of his called Henry, a great warrior, but utterly unscrupulous. Afterwards Henry had himself proclaimed King and he's ruled the Kingdom ever since. My brother and I escaped with great difficulty and managed to find asylum for Alfhild in a town called Brentford, where she's been ever since. But my brother and I went into hiding, and travelled from land to land calling ourselves Krak and Hrafn. With the help of our kinsmen we collected this fleet and army from various rulers. Henry has a lot of support from Scotland, being married to the daughter of Earl Melans of Moray, a close friend of Duncan, High King of Scotland, who founded Duncansby, and gave it his name. Now, Hrolf and Stefnir, I'd like to ask you to give me aid and support to avenge my father and win back my patrimony.'

'You're welcome to all the aid and support I can give you,' said Hrolf; 'and I won't part from you till either I'm a dead man, or you've won back your Kingdom and avenged your wrongs.'

Stefnir said very much the same, and Harald thanked them for their words of goodwill.

As soon as the feast was over, they got ready for a voyage, choosing all the bravest men. They left Bjorn the Counsellor in charge of the state and other notable men with him: but before they set out, Harald made a proposal of marriage and asked for the hand of Thora, Stefnir's sister. Hrolf and other great men pleaded on his behalf, and so it happened that Harald won her, though she was to wait for the marriage until he came back. After that they put out from Jutland with thirty well-fitted ships, and kept on sailing until they made landfall in England at a place

115

called Lindsey. They brought their fleet into an anchorage and lay there for several days waiting for a fair wind, having no wish to plunder there.

CHAPTER 36

The battle of Ashington

THE STORY GOES that King Henry had a man with him called Annis. He may have been old in years, but he knew about both the latest and the most ancient practices in wickedness and witchcraft. He'd fostered Henry and had always been his counsellor. Annis had told the King a month in advance about the arrival of Harald and Hrolf with a large force, and of what their plans were: he added that since Hrolf and Stefnir were great champions, subtle schemes were called for.

'If you take my advice', he said, 'you'll send messengers to Earl Melans, your father-in-law, in Scotland, and ask him to join you. Ask King Duncan to give you troops as well; and as soon as Hrolf's ashore, send a messenger to mark out the battlefield and challenge them to come there. Then, in accordance with correct viking law, they won't be allowed to plunder. The battlefield must be at Ashington, north of Kana Woods, where the terrain is roughest and hardest to escape through. Hide in the forest with half your troops, attack them from behind, and take them by surprise. Then we'll surround them, and none of them will get out alive.'

This seemed a good plan to the King, and he did everything Annis had proposed. Earl Melans came from Scotland with a large army, and Duncan sent King Henry another, led by two berserks called Amon and Hjalmar, big strong men and very tough. So now Henry's army seemed invincible. His messengers came to Lindsey and told Hrolf and his men that the field had been marked out for them at Ashington, and

116

that everything was ready for the battle. Some of Hrolf's men thought it unwise, in view of the huge army waiting for them, to venture so far inland with such a small force.

They sailed over to a place called Skorstein and left their ships there. Then they went ashore and marched without a break to Ashington. King Henry and Earl Melans were already there waiting for them with their invincible army, and hiding in the forest with a strong force were Amon and Hjalmar, though Hrolf and his men knew nothing about that.

So they formed up. King Henry deployed his men in three columns. He himself led the centre column and Earl Melans the second one. The third column was led by a count called Engilbert, a great champion, and with him a man called Raudam, tall, strong and very brave. Banners were carried before all the columns. Annis took no part in the battle. Harald decided to form up his own troops against King Henry, with Stefnir against Earl Melans, and Hrolf against Raudam and Engilbert.

After that the trumpets sounded, and both sides rushed into battle shouting encouragement. First there was an exchange of missiles, and then fierce hand-to-hand fighting, neither side showing any weakness. At first the Scots and the English were very keen, but the Danes hit back hard and fiercely. Early in the battle, just after it got started, Engilbert and Raudam went against Hrolf and attacked him both at the same time: but he defended himself well and bravely. He was wearing his armour with Vefreyja's cloak on top. Engilbert and Raudam were both agile and strong, and though Hrolf shattered all their protective armour, not a single blow could he land on their bodies. He began to tire, but thanks to his armour, no weapon could touch him. Then, as his rage mounted, this is what he did – he threw the sword away and flung himself with such violence at Count Engilbert that the count flew right up over his head and crashed down head first, breaking his neck.

At that moment Raudam made a two-handed stroke at Hrolf's back so hard the sword broke at the hilt. He tried to get Hreggvid's sword, but Hrolf rushed him and taught him which of them was the strongest, forcing him down and dashing his knee so hard against Raudam's chest that the ribs caved in. That was how Raudam and Engilbert died, and people thought them very brave men.

Now Hrolf picked up Hreggvid's sword, hewing left and right. The Scots found him a hard-hitter and fell back, but Hrolf didn't mind going after them, and killed everyone he could reach. Soon however the Danes realised that, no matter how hard their strokes, their weapons were failing even to bite armourless men. It was just as if they were hitting at them with sticks, though Hreggvid's sword kept biting as if it were cutting through water. As far as anyone knows, Grim Aegir was the only man ever to blunt that sword. The Danes now began to fall in greater numbers than the English.

Then they heard the loud blare of horns and a warcry. Running out of the forest with a large force of men came the berserks, taking Hrolf and his men completely unawares. The Danes began to fall in large numbers before the fierce attack. Hrolf told his men to face both ways, back to back. He himself supported the banner against the berserks. The battle was getting tougher. Stefnir fought a hard combat with Earl Melans. The Earl was a great warrior, and Stefnir's sword didn't bite at all. Amon and Hjalmar went against Hrolf. Together they struck at him, but he had his shield and defended himself vigorously. Then Hrolf swept with his sword at Hjalmar. The stroke landed on the thigh below the hip, slicing off the leg, and not long after that he died.

Then Annis stepped forward. He carried a shield as big as a door and in the other hand a small short-sword. Thrusting the short-sword at Hrolf's standard-bearer, he caught him in the belly, the sword passing clean through him, and the banner fell to the ground. Now that Annis had joined in the battle, the Danish weapons began to bite again. Men did all in their power, and there were huge losses on both sides, but the greater loss was among the Danes.

Wishing to avenge his standard-bearer, Hrolf struck at Annis. The

118

blow landed on the middle of the shield and split it down to the handle, where the sword stuck fast, but Annis had such a firm grip on the shield it didn't budge. Hrolf wanted to let go of the sword, but couldn't, for both his hands were stuck to the hilt.

Annis asked the Scots to give Hrolf his penance – 'now that the wolf's walked into the trap.'

And that's what they did, large numbers of them crowding about Hrolf, others hacking and raining blows on him. He was pelted with stones, hewn at with axes and battered with clubs. Hrolf glared at them in a rage and made things hard for them by lashing out with his feet, but he couldn't free himself.

Now we return to Stefnir, still fighting Earl Melans. His sword had begun biting again, and he struck at the Earl's helmet with all his strength, so hard that the blow split helmet, head, armour-clad trunk and all, and the sword finished up stuck in the ground. It had been a long fight.

Surprised not to see Hrolf or his banner anywhere, Stefnir began searching for him, and at last saw the trouble he was in. By now the attackers were trying to cut off Hrolf's feet, but Stefnir raced to his rescue, and took Annis by surprise, striking with his sword at his helmet rim and splitting it open, together with the whole of his face and both arms down to the elbows. That made Annis stagger. Now that Hrolf was free, getting in his way was no joke. As Amon turned to meet him, Hrolf struck him a double-handed blow on his shield and split it in two, and the point of the sword ripped open his chest and belly, so that the guts poured out and Amon fell dead. Hrolf was so angry he spared no one. He struck out as fast as hand can swing a sword, and three or four fell under each stroke. Men were being cut up like kindling at a charcoalburner's. Stefnir followed Hrolf's example, and the English began to fall in their hundreds.

King Henry and Harald had met early in the battle and had been fighting all day. By now, both of them were wounded and weakening,

119

but Harald much more so. Hrolf saw their struggle. Already he had been four times through King Henry's ranks and back again, and now he strode up to the King and struck at his spine, so that the King tumbled to the earth in two pieces.

Seeing that the King was dead, the Scots and the English began to run, each man as fast as his feet would carrying him, but the others routed them, killing everyone they caught who did not ask for quarter. Hrolf chased far after them, and once he got near them with his sword, there was no point in asking for mercy. A vast number of men died in the rout. Then the Danes turned back and stripped the dead, taking plenty of loot. Annis had been captured in the battle, and Hrolf had him torn apart by horses. That's how his life ended. Hrolf was badly wounded in the hands and feet, and all his body was black, bruised by the heavy blows, even though he hadn't been cut by them.

Harald and the others went over to Winchester, and the town surrendered to them. All the people of the land gladly gave themselves over to Harald, and he was made king over the whole land his father had once ruled. He gave Hrolf and Stefnir all the thanks they deserved for their support, their friendship, and their courage. The Scots who got away after the battle went back to King Duncan and told him about their defeat and the casualties they'd suffered. They said too that Hrolf was more giant than human in size and strength. Duncan took the losses he'd suffered very badly, but he just had to put up with them.

CHAPTER 37

Wedding feasts

HROLF AND STEFNIR spent the rest of the winter quietly with Harald. He sent to Brentford for his sister Alfhild, and she came with an elegant retinue of fair companions. Harald was as happy to see his sister as she to see him. Alfhild was a very beautiful and highly accomplished young woman just as a princess ought to be. Stefnir fell in love with her on the spot, and as soon as he began talking to her, she struck him as both intelligent and courteous. So Stefnir proposed to her, but she referred him to her brother. It was easy to plead with Harald, who already knew Stefnir to be a true gentleman and brave warrior. The outcome was that Alfhild was betrothed to Stefnir, and her dowry paid out by Harald in gold and treasure.

When spring came, they all got ready to sail back to Denmark and loaded their ships with malt, mead, wine, costly clothing, and all those goods that were most expensive in Denmark, but easy to get in England. Then they set course for Denmark, and Alfhild came with them. Everyone in Jutland was happy to have them back. The young women and Bjorn the Counsellor gave them a splendid welcome. Alfhild joined Ingigerd and Thora, and they all enjoyed themselves in one another's company.

Now they had their ships unloaded, and they prepared for a magnificent feast with all the best fare that could be got in Denmark or anywhere near. They spared nothing on halls or furnishings or anything that was to be found in Scandinavia. To this banquet they invited burghers and courtiers, counts and earls, dukes and kings, and everyone of any standing. Most of the nobility in Denmark were there, and when all of them had arrived and been shown to their seats, there were courteous young squires and the finest gentlemen to attend on them. All kinds of dishes were served there, spiced with the most precious herbs, and every sort of game and wild fowl, venison from deer and reindeer, pork from the best wild boars, geese, ptarmigans, and peppered peacocks. There was no shortage of glorious drink, ale and English mead, and the best of wines, both spiced and claret. And once the wedding and the banquet had begun, all kinds of stringed instruments, harps and fiddles, pipes and psalter, were to be heard. There was a beating of drums and a blowing of horns, with every variety of pleasant play to cheer the body of man. After that the two young ladies were escorted into the hall with a colourful train and cluster of splendid women. Two noblemen led by the hand each of the two ladies who were to marry the bridegrooms. Above them, supported on painted poles, was a canopy to conceal their resplendent clothing and elegance until they were seated. When the canopy was taken away, no colour, it seemed, could outshine their complexions, their skins, their gleaming hair, and all the glowing gold and jewels that they wore. Yet when they saw Ingigerd, everyone thought Alfhild and Thora pale by comparison. The banquet was held in all splendour, and during the feast Hrolf married Ingigerd, Stefnir Alfhild, and Harald Thora. The feast lasted seven days without a break, everything being arranged as we've just described, and it ended in honour and magnificence. The bridegrooms gave rare gifts to each of the noble guests, thanking them for their attendance, and afterwards, each went to his own home, full of praise for their host's magnanimity, all of them on the most friendly terms.

Each of the couples came to love one another dearly. King Harald didn't stay long in Denmark before getting ready to sail back home. He parted from his brother-in-law Stefnir and Hrolf the best of friends, and went back to his Kingdom. Queen Thora went with him, and they settled down quietly. They had children together, but their names aren't given.

England is the most productive country in Western Europe, because all sorts of metal are worked there, and vines and wheat grow, and a number of different cereals besides. More varieties of cloth and textiles are woven there than in other lands. London is the principal town, and then Canterbury. Besides these are Scarborough, Hastings, Winchester, and many towns and cities not mentioned here.

Stefnir was given the title of Earl over Jutland, and resided most of the time at Ribe. Denmark is a very disjointed country. Jutland, the largest part, lies southwards bordering on the sea. Jutland Side is the name of that part lying on the west coast from Skagen south to Ribe. There are several important towns in Jutland, Hedeby being the most southerly; another is Ribe, a third Aarhus, and Viborg a fourth, where the Danes choose their kings. Limafjord lies in Jutland stretching north to south, with Harald's Isthmus separating the head of the Fjord from the sea to the west. That's where King Harald Sigurdarson had his ships hauled across when he was fleeing from the attacks of King Svein.[1] West of Limafjord lies Skagen curving northwards, its main town being Jellinge. Between Jutland and Fyn stretches the Little Belt; the capital of Fyn is Odense. Between Fyn and Zealand is the Great Belt. Roskilde is the main town on Zealand. North of Zealand lies the Sound, and to the north of that, Skaane, with its main town of Lund. Between Jutland and Skaane are several large islands, Samso, Anholt, Laaland, and Langaland. The isle of Bornholm lies east in the Baltic. At that time the Skjoldungs ruled over this kingdom, and even though other kings and earls had realms just as large as theirs in Denmark, the Skjoldungs were held in greater respect because of their title and family.[2]

---

1. This is an allusion to an incident described in *Heimskringla* and elsewhere in the Kings' Sagas: 'King Harald sailed his ships farther up the fjord to its widest point, to a place called Livobredning; at the far end of the creek there, only a narrow neck of land separates the fjord from the North Sea. Harald and his men rowed there that evening; and during the night, under cover of darkness, they unloaded their ships and dragged them across the isthmus. Then they loaded the ships again and were ready to sail before dawn.' *King Harald's Saga* (Penguin Classics, 1966), p. 107.
2. The history of the Skjoldungs, the legendary kings of Denmark, was traced in *Skjoldunga Saga*, which is now lost apart from a single fragment and a Latin epitome made by Arngrimur Jonsson (1568–1648). References to the Skjoldungs occur in the Icelandic *Ynglinga Saga* (first part of Snorri Sturluson's *Heimskringla*, written *c*. 1230) Snorri's *Edda*, *Hrolf Kraki's Saga* and the Old English poem *Beowulf*. In the first nine books of his *Gesta Danorum*, Saxo Grammaticus (d. 1216) has a lot to say about these famous legendary kings.

CHAPTER 38

The saga ends

THE STORY GOES that Earl Stefnir didn't live long, and none of his children survived beyond childhood. Hrolf and Stefnir parted in great friendship and stayed good comrades for the rest of their lives. It's not known whether Hrolf ever went back again to Ringerike, but it's said that in the summer when Harald went west to England, Hrolf sailed with ten ships east to Novgorod, and Ingigerd with him. It's also said that Hrolf was adopted as king over the whole of Russia on the advice of the Princess and other important people.

One third of Russia is known as Kiev, and it borders on the mountain range which separates Russia from Giantland. Ermland and other small countries are thereabouts too.

Hrolf ruled his Kingdom with great distinction, being both wise and a good governor. Because of his power and courage, no chieftains ever dared to attack him. He and Ingigerd loved each other dearly, and had plenty of children. They had a son called Hreggvid, a man of great strength. He went on a viking expedition to the East, but never came back. According to learned men, Hrolf had another son called Olaf, that King of Denmark against whom Helgi the Brave waged war. But Hromund Gripsson supported Olaf, as told in his saga,[1] and killed

---

1. *Hromund Gripsson's Saga* survives in two versions. There is a metrical one composed in the fourteenth century (*Griplur*), on which a still later prose version is based. But this saga seems to have existed already in the early twelfth century. According to *The Saga of Thorgils and Haflidi*, a certain Hrolf of Skalmarness "composed" *Hromund Gripsson's Saga* to entertain the guests at a wedding feast at Reykholar in the west of Iceland in 1119. The same source also mentions that the saga was used to entertain King Sverri of Norway (1177–1202), who seems to have had a strong predilection for fantastic stories.

Helgi. Dagny and Dagbjort, the ones who healed Hromund, are said to have been Hrolf's daughters, but it isn't said whether or not they were Ingigerd's children. Hrolf's third son, called Hord, was father of Kari, father of Horda-Knut. The story goes that Hrolf lived to a ripe old age, but it's not stated whether he died in his bed or was killed with weapons.

Now even if there are discrepancies between this story and others dealing with the same events, such as names and other details, and what individual people achieved by greatness or wisdom or witchcraft or treachery, it's still most likely that those who wrote and composed this narrative must have had something to go on, either old poems or the records of learned men. There are certainly very few stories about ancient people, perhaps none, which one would like to swear to be the literal truth, because most of them have been more or less exaggerated. And it's impossible to prove the truth of every word and incident in some of the episodes, because most things described clearly occur later than they're supposed to. But it's best not to cast aspersions on this or call the stories of learned men lies, unless one can tell the stories more plausibly and in a more elegant way. Old stories and poems are offered more as entertainments of the moment than as eternal truths. There are few things told that can't be put in doubt by some old example to the contrary, and it's said in all truth that God has given the heathen wisdom and understanding of worldly things, along with outstanding bravery, wealth and physical beauty, just as he has Christians.

So here we must end this tale of Hrolf Sturlaugsson and his great exploits. I'd like to thank those who've listened and enjoyed the story, and since those who don't like it won't ever be satisfied, let them enjoy their own misery.

AMEN.

A bibliographical note

Göngu-Hrolfs Saga hasn't received the scholarly attention it deserves; the principal work on the tale is still Jakob Wittmar Hartman's *The Göngu-Hrolfs Saga. A Study in Old Norse Philology*, New York 1912. For other studies, see Halldór Hermannsson, *Islandica*, vols. V (1912) and XII (1937), and Hans Bekker-Nielsen, *Bibliography of Old Norse-Icelandic Studies*, 1963– (In progress).

References in the Introduction and footnotes are to the following translations:

Arrow-Odd. A Medieval Novel, tr. Paul Edwards and Hermann Pálsson, New York, 1971.
The Book of Settlements. (Landnámabók), tr. Hermann Pálsson and Paul Edwards, Winnipeg 1972.
Bosi and Herraud, see *Gautrek's Saga*.
Egil and Asmund, see *Gautrek's Saga*.
Eyrbyggja Saga, tr. Hermann Pálsson and Paul Edwards, Edinburgh 1973.
Gautrek's Saga and other medieval tales, tr. Hermann Pálsson and Paul Edwards, London 1968. Apart from the title story, the volume contains the following tales: *Bosi and Herraud*, *Egil and Asmund*, *Thorstein Mansion-Might* and *Helgi Thorisson's Story*.
Grettir's Saga, tr. Denton Fox and Hermann Pálsson, Toronto 1976.
Hedin and Hogni, tr. Eiríkr Magnússon and William Morris in their *Three Northern love stories, and other tales*, London 1875.
Hrolf Gautreksson, tr. Hermann Pálsson and Paul Edwards, Edinburgh 1971.

Hromund Gripsson, tr. Nora Kershaw in her *Stories and Ballads of the far past*, Cambridge 1921.

King Harald's Saga, tr. Magnus Magnusson and Hermann Pálsson, Harmondsworth, Middlesex 1966. See also Snorri Sturluson, *Heimskringla*.

Njal's Saga, tr. Magnus Magnusson and Hermann Pálsson, Harmondsworth, Middlesex 1962.

Olaf Tryggvason's Saga; see Snorri Sturluson, *Heimskringla*.

Orkneyinga Saga, tr. Hermann Pálsson and Paul Edwards, London 1978.

Saxo Grammaticus (d. 1216). *The first nine books of the Danish History of Saxo Grammaticus*, tr. Oliver Elton, London 1894.

Snorri Sturluson (d. 1241). *The Prose Edda of Snorri Sturluson. Tales from Norse Mythology*. Introduced by S. Nordal. Selected and translated by Jean I. Young, Berkeley 1964.

Heimskringla: History of the Kings of Norway, tr. Lee M. Hollander, New York 1964.

Sturla Thordarson (1214–84). *Hákon's Saga*, tr. Sir George W. Dasent, London 1888.

Sturlaug's Saga, tr. Otto J. Zitzelsberger in his *The Two Versions of Sturlaugs Saga Starfsama: A Decipherment, Edition and Translation of a Fourteenth Century Icelandic Mythical-Heroic Saga*, Düsseldorf 1969.

Thorstein Mansion-Might, see *Gautrek's Saga*.

Volsunga Saga, ed. and tr. R. G. Finch, London 1965.

Ynglinga Saga; see Snorri Sturluson, *Heimskringla*.